DOUBLE TAKE

Two sides One story

DESERT DUEL

To Lynne, with love

This story is based, as much as possible, on primary source material - the words and pictures of the people that witnessed the events described. Whilst it is not possible to know the exact thoughts, feelings and motives of all the people involved, the book aims to give an insight into the experience of the events, based on the available evidence.

Scholastic Children's Books
Commonwealth House, 1–19 New Oxford Street,
London, WC1A 1NU, UK
A division of Scholastic Ltd
London ~ New York ~ Toronto ~ Sydney ~ Auckland
Mexico City ~ New Delhi ~ Hong Kong

Published in the UK by Scholastic Ltd, 2004

ISBN 0 439 96790 2

Printed and bound by Nørhaven Paperback A/S, Denmark

Cover image supplied by Popperfoto

2 4 6 8 10 9 7 5 3 1

Contents

"Before Alamein we never had a victory. After Alamein we never had a defeat." *Winston Churchill*

BERNARD LAW MONTGOMERY was born in St Mark's vicarage, Kennington Oval, London on 17 November 1887. When Montgomery was two years old he and his family moved to Tasmania, a large island south-east of Australia. This was because Montgomery's father – a vicar – had been appointed Bishop of Tasmania. (At that time Australia, as well as India, Canada and much of Africa, were all part of what was known as the British Empire. Decisions about who governed these lands or was appointed to an official position were mainly taken in Britain.)

There is no doubt that Montgomery had an unhappy childhood – he says so himself in his memoirs. Montgomery's mother married his father when she was 16. She had nine children, of which seven survived. Montgomery's father was away from home a lot of the time, visiting parishes in different parts of Tasmania, and so the young Montgomery was left in the care of his mother, who bullied him and often beat him with a cane. Montgomery admitted that part of the problem may have been his own determined personality. Even as a young boy, Montgomery believed that he knew best, and this attitude brought him into conflict with people throughout his life.

During his time in Tasmania, Montgomery was educated at home by tutors who came from his native country. When the family returned to England in late 1901, Montgomery and his brother continued their education at St Paul's school in London. It was the first time Montgomery had ever been to school; he was 14 years old.

At St Paul's he showed great prowess at sports: in just over three years he became captain of the school's rugby XV and also played for the cricket team. However, he did not shine in academic subjects. A comment on his school report from 1905 reads: *"his essays are sensible but he has no notion of style."*

The impression we get from Montgomery's memoirs is that his childhood was a lonely one. He does not appear to have had any really close friends, even during his teenage years.

However, Montgomery decided early on that he wanted a career in the army, and in 1907 he sat the exam to enter the Royal Military Academy at Sandhurst. He gained a place, but found his time at the Academy difficult, surrounded as he was by students who came from wealthier backgrounds. Montgomery's parents were not well off, and he claims he was the poorest student at Sandhurst. Whether this was true or not, he certainly seemed to resent his peers.

When he passed out of the Academy in 1908 at the age of 21, Montgomery joined the British army in India. His reasons for this were purely financial: he could not afford to live in England on a Second-Lieutenant's pay, which was 5s 3d (26p) a day. This was at a time when, in Monty's own words:

A young officer could not possibly live on this income as his monthly mess bill [the bill for food] alone could not be less than £10.

In India he would get the same rate of pay, but be able to live on less money. In 1913, Montgomery returned to England for further training. By 1914, when the First World War broke out, he was a full Lieutenant. The War was between the Allies (including Britain and its Empire, France, Russia and Belgium) on one side, and Germany, Austria-Hungary and Turkey on the other.

Montgomery and his unit were sent to France, and took part in fighting on the Western Front at Mons and on the Aisne. Although the rifle was a vital part of each soldier's equipment, much of the fighting at this stage of the War was hand-to-hand combat, soldier against soldier, often using bayonets and swords.

In 1915, during an attack on a German position, Montgomery was shot through the chest by a sniper. As he lay on the ground he was shot through the legs. He was so badly wounded that the doctors said that he would not live, and a grave was even dug for him. However, when the time came for his unit to be moved, Montgomery was still alive, and so he was sent back to England to recuperate. He returned to the Western Front in 1916 as a Brigade Major.

Montgomery was deeply affected by his experiences in the early stages of the First World War. He had seen at first-hand how inefficient and disorganized the army was. Time and time again the only order he and his fellow soldiers were given was simply to rush forward at the enemy, with no reconnaissance, no plan, no covering fire. Mostly he was appalled by the lack of communication between the generals and the soldiers. In his memoirs he says:

> The higher staff were out of touch with the regimental officers and with the troops. The former lived in comfort, which became greater as the distance of their headquarters behind the lines increased... The so-called "good fighting generals" of the war appeared to me to be those who had a complete disregard for human life.

To illustrate his point, Montgomery tells the story of a top General who was returning to England after the heavy fighting on the Passchendaele Front during 1917 – 1918, near the end of the War. Before he went home, the General paid a visit to Passchendaele Ridge, where half a million men had died in the brutal conflict:

> *When he saw the mud and the ghastly conditions under which the soldiers had fought and died, he was horrified and said: "Do you mean to tell me that the soldiers had to fight under such conditions?" And when he was told that it was so, he said: "Why was I never told about this before?"*

Montgomery, was determined that this gulf between the Generals and the ordinary troops would not happen if he should ever be in the position of leading a campaign.

The First World War ended in victory for the Allies. Thinking about the huge loss of human life (four and a quarter million soldiers died, with a further ten million wounded), Montgomery decided that any future wars needed to be fought in a more intelligent way. Sheer brute force and strength of numbers weren't enough to guarantee success in the light of new methods of warfare. Military action needed planning if massive losses were to be avoided. And so in January 1920, after a further two years as a soldier, Montgomery returned to student life at the Army Staff College at Camberley where he studied the theory of war.

The Beginning

ERWIN JOHANNES EUGEN ROMMEL was born on 15 November 1891 at Heidenheim, near Ulm in Wurtenberg, southern Germany. His father was a schoolteacher, but as there was no primary school in the area where his father taught, Rommel did not go to school until he was nine years old. Like Montgomery, he was educated by private tutors, but he was not considered very bright. From Rommel's memoirs and letters we get the impression that, although his father was a stern and slightly aloof figure, Rommel himself had a happy boyhood and enjoyed playing games and sports with friends.

In 1910, at the age of 18, Rommel decided to join the army, and was sent to the Royal Officer Cadet School in Danzig. In 1912 he was commissioned as a Lieutenant in the 124th Infantry Regiment, and held this rank when the First World War began in 1914.

Rommel's men admired him because he always led an attack from the front, instead of organizing it from the rear, as many Officers did. In September 1914, while leading his platoon in an attack on French positions, he was seriously wounded after he ran out of ammunition for his rifle. He records:

I fired again – nothing. I whipped off the magazine to find it empty. The enemy were too close – no time to reload – and there was no cover to hand. My only hope lay in the bayonet. Although alone, facing three enemy soldiers, I had complete confidence in the weapon and my ability to use it. As I prepared to charge the enemy fired. I was thrown head over heels by the bullet to land five paces in front of my foe. A sideways shot had shattered my upper left leg. Blood spurted from a fist-sized wound. Every second I expected to be killed by bayonet or bullet. I pressed against the wound with my right hand while trying at the same time to roll to cover behind a tree. Then my men burst through the undergrowth and the enemy vanished.

The wounds Rommel sustained during this skirmish kept him out of action until January 1915. He returned to his battalion to find the nature of the war at the Western Front had changed. At the start of the War there had been brief confrontations between groups of armed soldiers, some of these between men on horseback armed with lances and swords. Now, in 1915, the beautiful countryside of France and Belgium had gone. In its place was a sea of mud, covered in miles of trenches and barbed wire. For the most part, the opposing armies remained in their trenches while their big guns fired shells at the other side. Sometimes attacks were launched from the trenches across areas of barbed wire, using rifles and bayonets. These attacks might result in winning just a few hundred yards of ground, only for the opposing side to retake those same few hundred yards a few days later.

Rommel was wounded again in July 1915. As a result of his bravery under fire, he was awarded one of Germany's highest military honours, the Iron Cross. After he had recovered from his wounds, he was transferred to a mountain battalion. In 1916 this battalion was sent to fight the Romanians, who had declared war on the Germany–Austria-Hungary Alliance. Rommel led a detachment behind the Romanian lines and captured vital enemy positions.

Italy had entered the war against Germany in 1915 and in October 1917 Rommel's mountain battalion was sent to the Alps to fight the Italians. This was to be one of his most successful actions of the War. Between 24 October and 10 November 1917, Rommel's unit helped destroy the Italian defences in the Alps. This included capturing the village of Longarone and taking 8,000 prisoners. For his outstanding actions, in 1917 Rommel was awarded Germany's highest military decoration, the *Pour le Merite* (also known as the Blue Max).

Italy's war against Austria-Hungary and Germany ended in disaster in 1917, with 600,000 Italian casualties. However, during 1918 Germany's defences began to crumble under the continuing onslaught of the Allied armies (including the Americans, who had entered the War in 1917.) As 1918 drew to a close, the Germans had to admit they were defeated, and they surrendered in November.

It was during the First World War, seeing the fighting at close hand, that Rommel developed his own theories of how a war should be fought. Like Montgomery, Rommel had observed that static battles – in which both sides just dug in and fired huge artillery shells at one another – led to large-scale loss of life on both sides. He believed this appalling and inefficient waste could be avoided, or at least reduced, if military units moved around at speed. Also, Rommel had come to believe that the power of a surprise attack could demoralize and paralyse an enemy. He believed this was a better tactic than spending time and resources on full-frontal attacks against strong defences. In Rommel's view, small well-trained and disciplined groups of soldiers could infiltrate enemy defences much more easily.

It would be over 20 years before Rommel got the chance to put his theories into practice.

The Years of Loss

MONTGOMERY GRADUATED FROM the Army Staff College in December 1920. From there he was sent as a Brigade Major to Ireland, where the Irish were fighting for their independence from Britain. Montgomery described this war as a "murder campaign" on both sides, and he hated his involvement in it. The War of Independence ended in 1922, with Ireland being split in two: the Irish Free State in the south and Northern Ireland, which remained part of the United Kingdom. After Ireland, Montgomery returned to the Army Staff College at Camberley, this time as an instructor. By 1926 he had risen to the rank of Lieutenant Colonel.

In 1927 Montgomery married Betty Carver, a widow who already had two children. Their son, David, was born in 1928. During much of their married life, Betty Montgomery accompanied her husband to foreign countries, such as Palestine, Egypt and India. Although they regularly visited countries where disease was rife, it was in England that tragedy struck. In 1937 Betty was playing on the beach with nine-year-old David at Burnham-on-Sea when she was stung on the foot by an insect. The poison from the insect bite spread and she became seriously ill. The doctors amputated her leg in a desperate attempt to stop the poison from spreading throughout her body, but it was too late and she died in October of that year. The death of his wife devastated Montgomery. He never married again, or even entered a serious relationship; instead he devoted himself completely to his army life.

Throughout the 1930s, Adolf Hitler, the German leader, was taking steps to make Germany the dominant power in the world. Under Hitler, Germany sought to expand its borders, beginning with the invasion of Czechoslovakia in March 1938. At first the British Government, headed by Prime Minister Neville Chamberlain, took no action except to enter into talks with Hitler on behalf of the countries threatened with German occupation. However, when Germany turned towards Poland, Britain delivered an ultimatum: if you invade Poland this will lead to a declaration of war. Hitler ignored this ultimatum and his troops entered Poland on 1 September 1939. As a result of this the British Government declared war on 3 September. The countries that formed the British Empire – Canada, Australia, India, New Zealand, South Africa, and the colonies in Africa and Asia – all pledged their military support to Britain in the fight against Hitler's Germany. These countries, together with France, Belgium, Poland, and all the others that opposed Hitler, became known as the Allies.

Chamberlain was sure that Hitler would not attack Britain directly, but Montgomery thought differently. Writing about a conversation he had with Chamberlain in December 1939, Montgomery says:

> *He took me aside and said in a low tone so that no-one could hear: "I don't think the Germans have any intention of attacking us. Do you?" I made it quite clear that in my view the attack would come at the time of their own choosing. It was now winter and we must get ready for trouble to begin when the cold weather was over.*

Montgomery was extremely angry about the way that the army had been reduced since the end of the First World War, as a result of cuts in the defence budget. In his opinion, the British army had been crucially weakened and was not ready to fight another war. However, as a professional soldier, he had to obey orders. In 1940 Major General Montgomery was put in charge of the 3rd Division and sent to Lille, on the French-Belgian border. His job was to support the Belgian defences against a possible German attack. Montgomery's first-hand experience in France led him to make fierce criticisms of the army:

> *The Field Army had an inadequate signals system, no administrative backing, and no organization for high command. The transport was inadequate and consisted of civilian vans and lorries. They were in bad repair and broke down constantly. It must be said to our shame that we sent our army into that most modern war with weapons which were quite inadequate. From the point of view of command and control of forces available in France in May 1940, the battle was really almost lost before it began.*

On 10 May 1940 the Germans launched an attack against Allied troops in Belgium and northern France. At first, Montgomery's 3rd Division and their Belgian comrades held their positions on the River Dyle at Louvain, withstanding the German attacks that were launched against them. However, on the night of 27 May, Montgomery was ordered to move his division forward and fill a gap in the Belgian front lines. As dawn broke the following day, he and his men were shocked to learn that the Belgian king had surrendered to the Germans only an hour before. Instead of being part of a defensive line, Montgomery and his soldiers were now isolated and in danger of being overwhelmed by the

German army. There was no choice left for Montgomery and his men but to retreat as quickly as possible to the French coast, and hope to get back to England.

Elsewhere, throughout Belgium and northern France, large numbers of Allied soldiers, overwhelmed by the better-equipped German forces, had been retreating to the northern coast of France. Since the middle of May, the retreating Allies had been ordered to gather at the Channel port of Dunkirk.

On 26 May 1940 a combined British, French, Dutch and Belgian fleet of ships set out to evacuate the troops to England, although with so many soldiers to be taken off the beaches, the task seemed almost impossible. In the harbour and on the open beaches of Dunkirk, more than 300,000 British, French and Belgian soldiers gathered and waited for the ships to come.

It took almost three days for Montgomery and his men to make the 100-mile journey to the French coast. They arrived just outside Dunkirk on the night of 30 May. By this time the fleet of ships taking the soldiers off the beaches had been going backwards and forwards across the English Channel for four days, all the time under a hail of heavy gunfire and bombing from German aircraft. In all, nearly a thousand boats, including fishing boats, lifeboats, small private yachts, ferryboats, even barges, in addition to ships from the Royal Navy, repeated the journey between Dunkirk and the English coast.

The RAF did its best to try and protect the fleet from the air attacks by the Germans, but they were heavily outnumbered by the Luftwaffe (the German air force). Also, the British planes could not carry enough fuel to stay over the French coast for very long.

Montgomery and those of his men who survived the attacks on the beaches managed to get on board a Royal Navy destroyer in the harbour at Dunkirk, and landed back in England at Dover on the morning of 1 June.

By 4 June, when the rescue operation (codenamed Operation Dynamo) had finished, 338,000 troops had been evacuated to England. About 22,000 British and 40,000 French had been either killed or taken prisoner. Many boats were lost in this operation. Two hundred of these were small crafts manned by British, French and Belgian volunteers. The Royal Navy also lost six destroyers. Around 2,000 men died in the boats that were lost at sea.

Despite the loss of life, the evacuation was considered a success. But Montgomery was angry at the way the public in Britain viewed what had happened at Dunkirk as "a victory of sorts":

I remember the disgust of many like myself when we saw British soldiers walking about in London with a coloured embroidered flash on their sleeve with the title "Dunkirk". They thought they were heroes, and the civilian public thought so too. It was not understood that the British Army had suffered a crushing defeat at Dunkirk and that our island home was now in danger of invasion. There was no sense of urgency.

Montgomery blamed the top brass in the military and the politicians for this appalling state of affairs. He was not known for keeping his opinions to himself, and he talked angrily to one of his comrades of the *"useless generals in charge of some of the Home Commands"*. This attitude made him unpopular with many of his superiors in the armed services, but there was one point they could not deny: Montgomery was an excellent soldier and commander of men. And later Montgomery was to have one very important supporter: Winston Churchill.

Unlike many British politicians of the time, Churchill had long spoken of the threat the German nation posed to the other European countries, including Britain. In 1940, Neville Chamberlain's government which had tried to maintain peace with Adolf Hitler, fell, and Churchill became prime minister. Churchill agreed with Montgomery that Britain was facing not only military disaster abroad, but also certain invasion. If decisive action was not taken soon, Germany would invade Britain – and the War would be lost.

The Rise of Germany

AFTER THE FIRST WORLD WAR the Allies had insisted on heavy cuts in the German army as a way of ensuring that Germany would never again be strong enough to fight a war. The German army was to have no more than 100,000 men. As a war hero and holder of the Blue Max, Rommel was one of the 400 Officers allowed to continue their careers in the army.

Because of these restrictions, the army did not have a great role to play. Much of Rommel's career between 1919 and 1934 was spent as an instructor at the Infantry School in Dresden.

In 1933, Adolf Hitler became the new Chancellor of Germany, and promised to make it the most powerful nation in the world, through politics and conquest. Rommel's view of Hitler's Nazi Party was mixed. Although Rommel himself was not a member at first he admired Hitler and his aim of making Germany great again. And in Rommel, Hitler saw a military Commander who could help him in this aim, and Rommel rose through the ranks, becoming a Colonel in 1938 and a Major General in 1939, in command of Hitler's official bodyguard.

It has been suggested that the admiration that Rommel and Hitler felt for one another came from the fact that both were from lower-middle-class families, and had worked their way up through the ranks. During their progress both had been made to feel inferior by the aristocrats who dominated the Officer class of the German army during the First World War.[1]

In February 1940 Rommel was appointed to command the 7th Panzer Division, one of the highly efficient tank units. On 10 May, during Germany's invasion of France, Rommel led the 7th Panzer Division into northern France.

At this stage of the War the number of troops on either side was slightly in favour of the Allies. They had 156 divisions, while the Germans had 136. The Allies also had greater superiority in tanks: 4,000 tanks compared to Germany's 2,800. The Germans' area of superiority was in the quality of their tanks and their tactics, but their greatest strength lay in the speed and surprise of their attacks – both on land and in the air. (It was a policy of

1 This was an experience that had also been shared by Montgomery in his early military career. In fact, the similarities at this point between Montgomery and Rommel were remarkable. Both were of the same generation, with just four years between their ages, and had started school later than was usual. Both had come from lower-middle-class families, and had risen through the Officer corps by ability, upsetting the ruling aristocratic Officer class in the military in the process. Both men had been seriously wounded during the First World War. Rommel and Montgomery were both Major Generals in their respective armies.

taking fast action based on collaboration between armoured divisions and the air force.)

Rommel put his theory about a fast-acting mobile force being able to defeat an enemy into effect, and soon his armoured divisions were rolling through road blocks set up by the Allies in north-eastern France. If they came up against a defence that was too strong, they simply went round it by a longer route and attacked it from the rear.

While other German divisions chased the retreating Allied troops towards Dunkirk, Rommel pushed on across northern France towards Cherbourg, on the Normandy peninsula that sticks out into the English Channel. The speed of his progress was incredibly fast; moving through the Ardennes, across the Somme and all those sites that had been the famous battlefields of the First World War just 20 years earlier. But it wasn't all plain sailing. Now and then Rommel's forces came up against stiff opposition, such as happened near Arras, where he was outnumbered by Allied tanks. In his journal, Rommel recorded:

I brought every available gun into action at top speed against these tanks. Soon we succeeded in putting the leading tanks out of action. A British captain climbed out of a heavy tank and walked towards us with his hands up. We had killed his driver. Despite a range of 1,500 yards the rapid fire of our anti-tank and anti-aircraft guns succeeded in bringing the enemy to a halt.

By June 1940, France had surrendered. Rommel's 7th Panzer Division had been the spearhead of the German attack, which had broken the spirit of the Allies with its speed and mobility. They had captured 90,000 Allied prisoners at a cost of 682 men dead and 1,646 wounded, and the loss of 42 German tanks.

Without either man being aware of the other's identity in these early battles in northern France, the first military encounter in which Montgomery and Rommel had both been involved had resulted in a victory for the German Commander.

Desert Hell

AFTER THE EVACUATIONS from Dunkirk, Montgomery was kept in charge of the 3rd Division. During the first part of June 1940, he prepared his men to return to the French battlefields to fight alongside the French. However, on 17 June, France surrendered and Montgomery's division was moved to the south coast of England to prepare for a likely invasion by German forces. It would remain there for the next two years.

On 10 July 1940, Italy entered the War on Germany's side. The combination of Germany and Italy was known as the Axis. (In 1940 Germany and Italy also signed the Tripartite Pact, a military alliance between themselves and Japan.) Following the success of Hitler's attack on Belgium and France, and the retreat of the British forces from Dunkirk, the Italian dictator, Benito Mussolini, was certain that he was throwing in his lot with the winning side, and was set on getting a share of world domination.

At that time Italy occupied Libya in North Africa, and Eritrea, Abyssinia, Ethiopia and Somaliland in North-East Africa. Sandwiched between Libya and Italian East Africa (as the other territories were known) were Egypt and the Sudan. These were independent countries but had "Protectorate Treaties" with Britain; this meant that if either Egypt or the Sudan was attacked by another country, then Britain would come to its aid.

With Italy entering the War on Germany's side, all British protectorates and territories in North Africa were at risk. It was vital that Egypt remained under Allied control if the Axis powers were to be defeated. Egypt had the biggest military base in the Middle East and it was the centre of a communications network with the rest of Africa, Australia, New Zealand, India and the Far East. Also in Egypt, at Alexandria (as well as at Haifa in Palestine), the Royal Navy held key harbours and repair facilities.

Whoever controlled Egypt also controlled the Suez Canal, one of the most important artificial waterways in the world. It connects the Mediterranean Sea with the Red Sea, and acts as a short-cut between Europe and the Arab countries. (Before the Suez Canal was built, ships had to make a long journey around the whole of Africa.)

The Mediterranean is at the hub of Europe, Africa and Western Asia. With the Germans and Italians in control of the European side of the Mediterranean, victory in

North Africa would give them complete control of the Mediterranean, and with Suez, control of the supply routes into each of the three continents.

In 1940 Italy had vastly superior numbers of troops in North Africa: 400,000 as opposed to the Allied force of 86,000. Of these 86,000 Allied soldiers (mainly British, Australian and South African), 36,000 were in Egypt, and they were short of equipment and ammunition. But it was obvious, just from the numbers alone, that the Italians would win any battle.

The enemy wasn't the only problem for the Allied troops in the desert; the conditions – the heat, the sand, the flies – were often unbearable.

One soldier with the 8th Army (the name given to the Allied army in North Africa), recorded that the soldiers were issued orders to kill at least 50 flies per man every day:

> *Eating and drinking became a work of art, one hand waving back and forth over the food, the other hand waiting, then a quick rush to the mouth before they pounced again. They were around our mouths, our eyes, our faces, anywhere there was moisture. They settled on the rim of hot cups of tea in dozens.*

Another soldier once counted 42 flies on his mug of tea. The sand, too, was all-invading. Bob Sykes, also from the 8th Army, described a sandstorm:

The sandstorm came at us like an express train at about 40 mph, with increasing gusts of wind. All oxygen seemed to go out of the air, and the flies were maddening and swarming. The heat was terrific and I sweated so the sand caked onto me – on my eyes, nose and ears. I sat down in my dugout and waited, thinking it would be over in a few minutes, but suddenly I panicked – the sand was coming through every crack. I thought I would be buried. I fought my way out... The sand was whipping the skin off my face and hands. It was almost pitch black and I felt entirely alone. Then a light appeared and the sun began to look a dirty orange. The noise slowly abated and the wind died down. I had ridden out my first sandstorm.

The sand was a major cause of damage to army vehicles, especially tanks. Dust clogged the filters of the tanks' engines and drastically reduced the distance the vehicles could cover before these filters needed to be replaced.

In September 1940 the Italians launched their attack against the much smaller Allied forces. Faced with overwhelming odds, the Allies, under the command of Major General O'Connor, made a fighting withdrawal to a defensive line at a place called Marsa Matruh and dug in.

The overall Commander of the Allied forces in Egypt, General Wavell, decided to launch a counter-attack against the Italians. In early December he ordered O'Connor and 30,000 men to attack. By 12 December, they had taken 38,000 Italian prisoners (including four Generals), 237 guns and 73 tanks. Throughout December 1940 and January 1941, O'Connor's forces continued to advance, forcing Italian troops to surrender in large numbers, the last of them surrendering on 6 February 1941. In just two months, O'Connor's force, with a total strength of 30,000 men had advanced 500 miles. They had destroyed the Italian army in North Africa, taking 130,000 Italian prisoners, and capturing 400 tanks and almost 1,000 guns. It had been a major triumph for Wavell, and especially for O'Connor.

Meanwhile, back in England, Montgomery continued to prepare the south coast of Britain for the expected German invasion from across the Channel. He had been promoted from his position as Commander of the 3rd Division, and by early 1941 had been put in charge of the whole south-coast stretch from Dorset to Kent.

Although Montgomery would have preferred to be where the fighting was taking place – in Africa or mainland Europe – as a loyal soldier, he was determined to carry out his orders with the greatest skill and determination. His job was to prepare England against invasion, and he was going to make sure that the troops who made up his defences were as fit and as tough as it was possible to be. He set up strict exercise programmes and made his men train in all conditions, good weather and bad. He set up practice situations where some of the men pretended to be German invaders and others acted as the defenders. Montgomery was determined that if and when the invasion came, his defending force would not give in easily. His slogan was: *"Total war demands total fitness from highest to lowest."* This also applied to his Officers. Commanders and Staff Officers who couldn't stand the strain of Montgomery's training routines were weeded out and replaced.

Montgomery's dedication brought him to the attention of the new prime minister, Winston Churchill. Churchill came to visit Montgomery and watched his troops in action during one of their exercises. He was very impressed by their professionalism and toughness. He listened as Montgomery outlined his ideas on military strategy for the defence of Britain. Up until then, the military top brass had advocated a "scorched-earth" policy in the event of an invasion. After the Germans had landed, as they advanced inland towards London, the retreating British troops would burn and destroy the countryside as they went. Montgomery's view was the exact opposite of this. He maintained that there should be no retreat. The British troops defending the coast should be strong enough to stop the Germans from advancing inland. Montgomery felt that the way to do this was to hit the invaders hard as soon as they landed, when they were still feeling weak from the sea crossing. The defensive line should also be constantly moving, because the Germans had shown in France that they could get around stationary trench-like defences. The defending force had to be mobile and be able to move to wherever the Germans were trying to break through, and attack them with heavy gunfire.

Churchill went away from his meeting with Montgomery aware that he had found a General who shared his own view of how to fight this war: not by retreating, but by aggressive fighting tactics; to stop the enemy in its tracks, and then destroy them. In Montgomery, Churchill thought he had found a General who could perhaps win this war for the Allies.

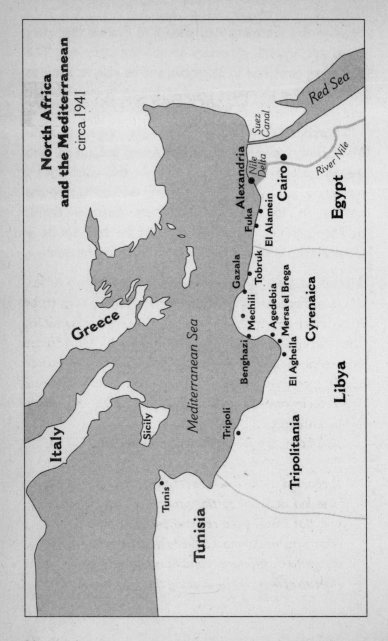

North Africa and the Mediterranean circa 1941

Rommel
The Desert Fox Strikes
February 1941 – July 1942

HITLER WAS FURIOUS at the Italian defeat in North Africa. Victory there was vital if the Mediterranean was to be kept under the control of the Axis countries. Following the surrender of the Italian troops, Hitler offered Mussolini the assistance of a whole German armoured division, on the condition that the Italians did not retreat from their remaining stronghold in Libya, at Tripoli. Mussolini agreed.

On 6 February Rommel was summoned to Berlin.

I reported to the Fuehrer [Hitler], who gave me a detailed account of the situation, and informed me that I had been recommended to him as the man who would most quickly adapt himself to the altogether different conditions of the African theatre of war. In the evening the Fuehrer showed

> *me a number of British and American illustrated*
> *papers describing General Wavell's advance*
> *through Cyrenaica [the eastern side of Libya*
> *where it bordered with Egypt]. Of particular*
> *interest was the masterly co-ordination these*
> *showed between armoured land forces, air and*
> *navy.*

On 11 February Rommel arrived in Rome to receive his detailed orders. These were to assist the Italians in the defence of Tripoli, and to keep a small reconnaissance force in that area. Rommel was told that he would be under the command of the head of the Italian forces. He was also ordered not to launch any key attack against the Allies until his 15th Panzer Division landed in North Africa. They were not expected until mid-April.

Rommel then flew to Sicily to meet the area Commander of the Luftwaffe, General Geissler. He learned from him that the Italian forces in North Africa were completely and utterly demoralized. Wavell's troops had taken Benghazi, a major town on the Libyan coast, and had destroyed the last Italian armoured division south of the town. They were about to advance into Tripolitania (the western side of Libya where it bordered Tunisia). No further serious resistance by the Italians was expected.

Rommel knew that something had to be done at once to bring the Allied offensive to a halt. He asked General Geissler to attack the port of Benghazi that night, and to send bombers the next morning to attack the Allied columns south-west of the town. At first General Geissler refused; apparently the Italians had asked him not to bomb Benghazi as many Italian Officers and civil officials owned houses there. Rommel was furious when he heard this excuse and contacted Hitler's HQ the same night to get the authority to go ahead with the attack. A few hours later the first Axis bombers took off on their mission to attack Benghazi.

The next day Rommel flew to Libya. There he received detailed reports of the recent Italian defeat. It was not a pretty picture. The retreat by the Italians had not been conducted in an orderly military fashion, but in utter chaos, with every man running for his life. Many Italian troops had thrown away their weapons and clambered on to overloaded vehicles in a wild attempt to escape to the west. This had led to some ugly scenes, with some of the Italian soldiers even shooting one another in their efforts to board a vehicle and get away. Morale was as low as it could be. Rommel was told that most of the Italian Officers had already packed their bags and were hoping for a quick return to Italy. Even the Commander of the Italian forces, General Garibaldi, thought the situation was lost, and showed little enthusiasm for Rommel's plan to establish a defence. Rommel realized that things were so bad that he had to take drastic steps:

> *I had already decided, in view of the tenseness of the situation and the sluggishness of the Italian command, to depart from my instructions to*

confine myself to reconnaissance and to take command at the front into my own hands as soon as possible, at the latest after the arrival of the first German troops.

Rommel's first aim was to stop Wavell's advance. The problem was that he had limited resources at his disposal; only 60 Italian tanks at this point, and they were so old, and their technology so out of date that they were almost useless against the modern tanks being used by the Allies. Rommel realized that the only means he had of holding the Allies back was the Luftwaffe, and so he ordered them to begin bombing Wavell's forces day and night.

In an effort to make the Axis forces appear stronger than they actually were (and to ensure the Allies remained cautious and didn't launch a sudden attack against his forces), Rommel carried out a piece of masterly cunning. He ordered the Axis workshops south of Tripoli to produce large numbers of dummy tanks made from wood. These were mounted on cars and driven around the desert where they kicked up lots of sand. From the air, Allied planes reported that the Axis had a huge force of tanks in the area, which appeared to be massing for an attack. Along with the constant heavy bombing, the ruse worked. General Wavell's army stayed put at El Agheila.

On 24 February Rommel sent out a German battalion and an Italian column with orders to "engage the enemy". It was a small but morale-boosting victory for the Axis forces. Without suffering any casualties themselves, they destroyed two enemy scout vehicles, a truck and a car, and took three Allied soldiers prisoner, among them an Officer. Meanwhile, other Axis units continued to advance towards the Allied positions. To guard against any Allied counter-attacks, they planted landmines in the area before returning to their own lines. In fact, no Allied counter-attack came, which made Rommel wonder if the Allies were weaker than he had been told.

Rommel was keen to push forward and take the advantage. Unfortunately for him, he was also still under orders from Berlin not to mount a major attack until his main force – the 15th Panzer Division – arrived in North Africa during April. What Rommel did not know was that at this time Hitler was planning Operation Barbarossa, the invasion of the Soviet Union. Hitler did not want the campaign in North Africa using up supplies that would be needed on the Russian Front, and so Rommel did not receive the men and equipment he wanted.

On 19 March an angry Rommel flew to Berlin to demand more support, only to be told by the top German military Commanders that there was no intention of striking a decisive blow in Africa in the near future, and that for the present he could expect no reinforcements.

Rommel was told that after the arrival of the 15th Panzer Division, which had been delayed and was now scheduled for the end of May, he was to attack and destroy the enemy around Agedebia (an inland town 100 miles south of Benghazi) and also the town of Benghazi itself. Rommel pointed out that if he took Benghazi he would have to occupy the whole of Cyrenaica, as the Benghazi area could not be held by itself, and for this he would need reinforcements. Rommel was deeply unhappy at the decision by his senior Officers not to let him have the extra number of troops he wanted for his campaign. Later he observed: *"The momentary weakness of the British should have been exploited with utmost rigour, so as to take the initiative at the outset."*

Rommel returned to North Africa, angry and frustrated, but determined to press on with launching an offensive against the Allies. Before his departure he had given instructions to prepare an attack on El Agheila, with the object of taking the airfield and small fort, and driving out the Allied troops. In the early hours of 24 March, a German reconnaissance battalion launched an attack against the fort. The front-line Allied forces defending the garrison were only small, but they had been waiting for such an attack. They had already mined the whole place and now withdrew in face of the German assault. Once the Germans had dealt with the mines, they were left in command of the fort, the airfield, and the all-important well, the source of vital water supplies.

Reports from reconnaissance flights by the Luftwaffe told Rommel that after retreating from El Agheila, the Allies had assembled on a high ridge at Mersa el Brega, about 45 miles away. There they had begun to gather reinforcements. Although Rommel had been instructed not to launch a major attack until May, all his instincts as a warrior told him not to wait.

> *I was faced with the choice of either waiting for the rest of my troops to arrive at the end of May – which would have given the British time to construct such strong defences that it would have been very difficult for our attack to achieve the desired result – or going ahead with our existing small forces to attack and take Mersa el Brega in its present undeveloped state. I decided for the latter.*

In defiance of his orders from Berlin, Rommel launched his attack on 31 March. There was a fierce battle and, in the face of the ferocious German onslaught, the Allies began to retreat towards Agedebia. It was a chance Rommel could not resist and on 2 April he gave orders for Agedebia to be attacked and taken. The Allies had laid only small minefields there and the Germans were able to deal with them without too much trouble as they made their advance. At the same time, Italian forces moved towards the town along the coast roads. The combined Axis forces took Agedebia in the afternoon and then continued advancing, the forward units pushing on as fast as they could.

On 3 April Rommel moved his HQ forward to

Agedebia and watched the Allies retreat. That day the delighted Rommel wrote to his wife.

> *Dearest Lu. We've been attacking since the 31st with dazzling success. There'll be consternation amongst our masters in Tripoli and Rome, perhaps in Berlin too. I took the risk against all orders and instructions because the opportunity seemed favourable. No doubt it will all be pronounced good later and they'll say they'd have done exactly the same in my place. We've already reached our first objective, which we weren't supposed to get to until the end of May. The British are falling over each other to get away. Our casualties are small.*

The speed and cunning with which Rommel led his campaign in the desert resulted in him being known by the Allies as "The Desert Fox".

However, Rommel's actions did not go down well with General Garibaldi, who was officially Rommel's superior Officer. A meeting between the two men turned into a furious argument when Garibaldi insisted that Rommel's aggressive operations against the Allies were in direct contradiction to orders from Rome. Garibaldi ordered Rommel to stop all action and undertake no further moves without his express authority. Rommel was just as angry and retorted furiously that he intended to go on doing what he felt he had to in whatever situation might arise. In the middle of this confrontation a message arrived from the German High Command giving Rommel complete freedom of action and settling the argument exactly as he wanted it.

The Allies tried to dig in against the advancing Germans at the town of El Melichi, but the fierceness of the German onslaught coupled with their own depleted numbers forced them to retreat still further to the town of Derna. A "last stand" at Derna turned into a major victory for Rommel, as we can see from his diary:

8 April 1941. We managed to reach Derna by 1800 hours where Ponath [a Lieutenant-Colonel in charge of a battalion] reported the capture of 800 British prisoners, including to my great joy almost the whole of the British staff.

Part of the 15th Panzer Division had just arrived in Africa. Rommel now instructed its Commander, General von Prittwitz, to take command of the pursuit force and follow the Allies to Tobruk, a town on the Libyan coast.

Wavell had ordered part of his retreating forces to gather at Tobruk intending to make a strong defence against Rommel's advance. For the next six months, Tobruk was a town under siege, as Rommel launched attack after attack in an attempt to defeat Wavell's forces, but to no avail. Cut off from help by land, the Allied troops in Tobruk depended on supplies of food and ammunition being brought in by sea. The boats that carried the supplies came under heavy attack from Axis aircraft and ships, but they managed to get through and keep the troops alive.

Meanwhile, the rest of Rommel's forces pushed the retreating Allied forces back to the Egyptian border.

In July 1941 Wavell was replaced as Commander-in-Chief of the Allied forces in North Africa by Field Marshal Auchinleck. Auchinleck decided he needed to build up his defensive position on the Egyptian border before launching an attack on the Axis forces. Then, on 18 November 1941, Auchinleck launched the "Crusader Offensive". During a series of fierce battles lasting a month, Auchinleck's men forced Rommel's army to retreat across all the territory he had won, right back to El Agheila. At the same time the siege of Tobruk was lifted and Allied troops were finally reunited with their comrades.

In January 1942, Rommel launched his own counter-attack, and the Allied forces were in turn forced back to Gazala by April. On 26 May, Rommel launched an attack on the Allied positions at Gazala. By late June, the Allied forces, heavily defeated, were forced to withdraw into Egypt. Rommel's advancing army attacked the garrison at Tobruk on 21 June, this time taking 35,000 Allied prisoners and a haul of supplies, which Rommel's forces were much in need of.

By 30 June 1942 Rommel's forces were facing El Alamein, a coastal town in Egypt where the Allied forces had dug in, about 50 miles west of Alexandria. After his latest series of victories, Rommel was convinced that all he needed was just one last push, one last victory, and the War in North Africa would be over.

Montgomery
"No Withdrawal"
August 1942

AMERICA HAD come into the War after the Japanese air force had launched an attack on the American naval fleet at Pearl Harbour in the island of Oahu in Hawaii on 7 December 1941. Two thousand four hundred servicemen were killed in the Japanese raid. Up until this time America had remained neutral in the War, but now, on 8 December, America declared war against Japan and its allies, Germany and Italy. Hitler retaliated by declaring war on the USA on 11 December.

In July 1942 a joint operation was being planned, combining both American and British forces, to land in North Africa in November that year. This operation was codenamed "Operation Torch", and was to be led by General Eisenhower on the American side, and General Montgomery on the British side. Montgomery was delighted to be relieved of the job of preparing Britain's defences in the event of a German invasion. At last he was to be involved in the real action.

The plan was to push the Axis forces out of North Africa completely. It depended on the Allied 8th Army defeating Rommel's forces at El Alamein and pushing them westwards, back from Egypt. At the same time Operation Torch forces would be moving eastwards. Rommel's troops would be caught in a pincer movement from both sides. Rommel would then either have to surrender, or retreat and take his forces across the Mediterranean to Italy. But the news from North Africa in July 1942 wasn't good. At El Alamein the Allied forces were digging in, while Rommel was bringing up reinforcements and more supplies in preparation for another attack.

In London, Churchill and the top military Commanders realized that drastic measures were needed if the situation in North Africa was to be saved. On one occasion Churchill was heard to exclaim in angry frustration: *"Rommel, Rommel, Rommel! What else matters but beating him?"*

Field Marshal Auchinleck was determined to do everything he could to prevent Rommel launching an attack at El Alamein. He realized that Rommel's one weakness was the length of his supply lines. All Rommel's supplies had to come by boat from Italy then be flown by large transporter planes, or brought by fleets of lorries, across the desert from the Libyan ports, such as Tripoli, Benghazi and Tobruk. Since the end of July Auchinleck had asked the RAF to shift the main weight of its bombing to attack these supply lines. The Luftwaffe wasn't able to defend the Axis supply lines properly because all its strength was needed to fight increasing numbers of Allied aircraft at the battle front. The attacks by the RAF on Rommel's supply lines dramatically slowed down preparations for his big attack.

Despite Auchinleck's success, the Allies decided to change the command in North Africa again. Field Marshal Alexander was sent out to replace Auchinleck as Commander-in-Chief of the Allied forces. Lieutenant General Gott was given command of the 8th Army.

As well as units from England, Scotland, Wales and Northern Ireland, the 8th Army included brigades from South Africa, Australia, New Zealand, India and Rhodesia. It also contained divisions of French soldiers who were part of the Free French Army, as well as American volunteers with the King's Royal Rifle Corps.

At the start of August 1942, all the parts of Operation Torch seemed to be in place. However, on his way to Cairo to take up his post as Commander of the 8th Army, Gott was killed when his plane was shot down.

On 8 August at about 0700 hours, the War Office telephoned Montgomery and told him the orders issued the previous day about leading Operation Torch had been revoked. He was to go to Egypt at once to take command of the 8th Army in the desert. Montgomery was delighted. He recorded in his journal:

I was to take command of an army which was at grips with a German and Italian Army under the command of Rommel – of whom I had heard great things. It was true that I had never fought in the desert and I would have under me some very experienced generals who had been out there a long time. However, Rommel seemed to have defeated them all, and I would like to have a crack at him myself.

On the same day that Montgomery was flying to Egypt, 8 August, Allied bomber planes attacked the port of Tobruk, destroying the main wharf. This cut the port's capacity by 20 per cent. It was a major blow to Rommel's supply lines.

As Montgomery flew to Egypt to take up his post, he read through the reports of the battles that had taken place so far, trying to work out a plan. From what he had read and heard, Rommel's forces consisted of holding troops (who manned static defence positions and held vital areas of ground) and mobile troops (who were used for counter-attacks and to form the spearhead – the attacking front line – of offensives). The holding forces were largely made up of Italians and were mostly unarmoured – that is, they did not have tanks or armoured vehicles. The mobile forces were German and, for the most part, armoured vehicles. Among these were Rommel's elite mobile forces, the Panzer divisions.

The more Montgomery read about Rommel's successes against the Allies, the more he realized that the 8th Army needed an equivalent of Rommel's Panzers:

> ... *a corps strong in armour, well equipped, and well trained. It must never hold static fronts; it would be the spearhead of our offensive. Because of the lack of such a corps we had never done any lasting good. The formation of this corps of three or four divisions must be a priority task.*

On arriving in Egypt, Montgomery discussed his plans with his Commander, Field Marshal Alexander, and the Deputy Chief of Staff, General Harding. He asked them if it was possible to form this new corps from the tanks and men scattered around Egypt. Montgomery knew that 300 new Sherman tanks were due to arrive in Egypt, coming through the Suez Canal from America, on 3 September, and he thought that these could provide the vehicles for his new armoured divisions. Harding agreed at once. The new division would be called the 10th Corps and would consist of three armoured divisions. Each of these divisions would be made up of one armoured brigade (tanks), one infantry brigade (fighting foot soldiers), plus support troops. Finally, the 10th Corps would have a New Zealand division made up of two infantry brigades and one armoured brigade.

On 13 August 1942, with his own "Panzer Division" being prepared, Montgomery then travelled to the 8th Army's desert headquarters.

The sight that met his eyes was appalling. It was a desolate scene: a few trucks, no mess tents (where food was usually served), work being done mostly in trucks or in the open air in the hot sun, flies everywhere. When he asked why there were so few tents, he was told that earlier Commanders had forbidden them in the 8th Army: everyone was to be as uncomfortable as possible so that the men couldn't complain that the Officers were getting preferential treatment. All meals were served in the open air where, of course, they attracted the flies.

I told them I did not like the atmosphere I found at Army HQ. No one could have a high morale in such a dismal place as this, living in such discomfort. The order forbidding tents was cancelled. Let tents and mess furniture be got and let us all be as comfortable as soon as possible.

On the first day of his command Montgomery assembled all the Officers. He issued orders that in the event of enemy attack there would be NO withdrawal. He famously said that the 8th Army would fight on the ground they now held *"and if we can't stay here alive we'll stay here dead"*.

He explained that his "no withdrawal" order involved a complete change of policy. If the 8th Army was to fight where it stood then the defences had to be much better organized. Ammunition, water, rations, etc, had to be stored in forward areas to make sure the front-line troops had these vital supplies at hand. More troops were needed in the front line to make the order possible. Montgomery pointed out that there were plenty of troops back in Egypt who were getting ready to defend Alexandria and the Suez Canal if El Alamein fell, but he felt that this was a defeatist attitude. He said that the only way to fight Rommel was to put more troops at the front at El Alamein and stop the Axis forces getting any further into Egypt. To do this, he intended to bring the reserve troops, who were deep inside Egypt, up to the front line.

Montgomery went on to tell the Officers that his orders from Field Marshal Alexander were quite simple: they were to destroy Rommel and his army. All the intelligence reports showed that the Axis forces were expected to launch an attack against the Allied position at El Alamein very soon. It was Montgomery's opinion that if Rommel launched his attack within days then defending El Alamein could be difficult, as there would be no time for Montgomery to organize the defences as he would like. He needed at least a week to ensure everything was in order. But he also informed his Officers that whatever Rommel did, he had no intention of launching his own attack against the Axis forces until he felt the 8th Army were ready and could follow the attack through and push Rommel's forces right out of Africa.

Montgomery left his assembled Officers in no doubt at all that the man who had been put in charge of them was determined to put his own stamp on the 8th Army, and on the war in North Africa.

During his first days at 8th Army HQ, Montgomery had discovered that the Air Force HQ was many miles back on the sea shore. Montgomery said afterwards that at this stage he felt the army and the air force appeared to be fighting two separate battles, without the essential close relationship between the two forces. He claimed later that it was he who set about forming a chain of communications between the two in order to co-ordinate military actions.

However, Auchinleck fiercely disputed this view. As we have already seen, the RAF had carried out major bombing raids against the Axis forces in co-operation with Auchinleck. Wavell, too, had made sure that the land and air forces worked together. It is said that Montgomery liked to be thought of as the originator of all ideas – he may have thought it would help his reputation if he was seen as the man who had won the battle for the desert after all others had failed.[2]

In his memoirs, Montgomery wrote about the huge task in front of him:

I knew I could not tackle it alone. I must have someone to help me, a man with a quick and clear brain who would accept responsibility and who would work out the details and leave me free to concentrate on the major issues.

2 In later years there was much bitter disagreement between Montgomery and Auchinleck over how effective the latter had been as the Commander in the desert. Certainly, at the start of his time there, Montgomery seemed to go out of his way to highlight Auchinleck's failings.

Montgomery needed a Chief of Staff and the man he chose for this job was Freddie de Guingand. It was a surprising decision as the two men were complete opposites. Montgomery was a non-smoker with a strong dislike of alcohol – a very controlled and cautious man who kept his emotions to himself. De Guingand, on the other hand, was described by Montgomery as *"highly strung, quite temperamental"*. In civilian life, de Guingand enjoyed fine wines, good food and cigars. He also liked gambling. But Montgomery decided these differences between them did not matter. He knew that de Guingand had a clever, analytical mind and trusted him to see that his orders were carried out by the Commanders, and to give him honest opinions in their discussions about strategy.

De Guingand's role wouldn't stop at this. He would also gather information and take reports from Montgomery's Officers while his Commander slept. Montgomery always insisted on getting a full night's sleep to be fresh for decision-making, even if a battle was taking place. He gave orders that once he was asleep he was not to be disturbed under any circumstances and that all reports should be made to his Chief of Staff. This order was only disobeyed once – in Montgomery's early days in the desert, when he was woken up soon after dawn by an Officer with a situation report. Montgomery was extremely angry and told the Officer that no one was ever to come near him with situation reports but to make all reports to his Chief of Staff. If anything was wrong the

Chief of Staff would tell him. If nothing was wrong he didn't want to be told.

Having appointed de Guingand, Montgomery spent the next few days inspecting the immediate area around El Alamein. He saw at once the importance of two dominating areas of ground: the Ruweisat and the Alam Halfa ridges. Although both were important, he felt the key to the Alamein position was Alam Halfa because of its high position overlooking the whole area.

Rommel's favourite tactic was to lure the Allied tanks from under cover to attack the Axis forces. He achieved this by sending out a small tank force and armoured vehicles to attack the Allies. This small force then retreated and the Allies usually sent out a larger number of tanks after them. When this happened, Rommel hid his small force behind a screen of anti-tank guns, which then knocked out the Allied tanks.

Whatever happened, Montgomery decided that he would not allow his tanks to rush out against the enemy. Instead they would stand firm in the Alamein position, hold the Ruweisat and Alam Halfa ridges securely, and let Rommel beat up against them:

> *I was determined to make our position at Alamein so strong that we could begin preparations for our own great offensive and not become preoccupied by any attack that Rommel might decide to make.*

All the information that had been gathered seemed to suggest that Rommel would attack towards the end of the month in the full-moon period. Most Generals preferred to launch an attack at night, hoping to catch their opponents while most of their troops were sleeping. The full moon was vital because it gave the light needed for the infantry to see the enemy.

If this information was correct, Montgomery had just over two weeks to prepare his defences.

The Battle of Alam Halfa

August – 6 September 1942

ROMMEL HAD SPENT the months following his successful onslaught on the Allied forces replenishing supplies, repairing equipment and bringing up fresh troops. However, he was aware that the Allied forces would be doing the same. In his journal he recalled:

> *We reckoned on mid-September as the date when the 8th Army's reinforcements would arrive. Once that happened the balance of strength would then be so heavily against us that our chances of mounting an offensive would be gone for good. So we intended to strike first.*

Rommel's intention was to launch an attack that would go around the Allied position and then head at speed towards the Nile Delta, where the River Nile branched out and flowed into the Mediterranean. Rommel was convinced that if he could get to the Nile, he could continue his advance and push right on to the vital sea-link that was the Suez Canal.

There were other reasons why Rommel had to get his attack launched as quickly as possible. Every day that passed the Allies laid more and more mines along their front. Rommel's original plan had been to attack using an outflanking move, in which his troops attacked the Allies from both sides. However, as the Allied front line grew longer, it meant that if he used this method of attack, his forces would be dangerously thinned out, and would be vulnerable to Allied attack from the centre. To keep his forces as near to each other as possible so they could give each other support, it would mean pushing some of his troops through the centre of the Allied front line. But Rommel was worried when he saw that the previously weak Allied front line appeared to be getting stronger day by day.

The Luftwaffe reported that several large convoys had arrived in the Suez Canal during July, bringing several hundred thousand tons of supplies for the Allied forces in Egypt. Meanwhile, as we have seen, Rommel was having serious problems with his own supplies coming under constant attack by the RAF.

Supplies for the Axis forces in North Africa came from Italy, and Rommel felt angry at the way in which the Italian forces were given priority over the Germans. While many of the Italian units in the Alamein front line were being supplied with new vehicles at speed, not one German replacement vehicle left Italy for the Afrika Korps (the name given to the combined Axis force in North Africa) up to the beginning of August. This was particularly annoying for Rommel as the Afrika Korps contained approximately two Germans for every one Italian (82,000 Germans to 42,000 Italians). During the month of August the supplies shipped across the Mediterranean by Marshal Cavallero, the Chief of the Italian High Command, were 8,200 tons for the German units and 25,700 tons for the Italian units. This suggested definite favouritism towards the Italians.

Not only were Rommel's supplies low, but the unloading of ships in the African ports, by the mainly Italian workers, was a disorganized process, partly because of RAF bombing. Rommel made repeated demands for increased port construction in the towns along the North African coast to help speed up the delivery of supplies, but with little success. Rommel believed that one major cause of these difficulties was the political relationship between Germany and Italy. Germany was trying to keep Italy happy and this prevented Rommel complaining to the Italian High Command about the Italian workers' weaknesses, and demanding that they be put right.

Supplies weren't Rommel's only problem. Seventeen thousand of the Germans in the Afrika Korps had been in action in Africa since the beginning of the campaign, and all of them had suffered severely from the effects of the climate. Rommel had no choice but to send them back to Germany. In a report he stated:

> *Much as I regretted losing these battle-tried veterans I was forced to ask for their relief, since by far the majority of them were no longer usable in a crisis. The German divisions were short of a further 17,000 men caused by death, sickness and wounds.*

Given the situation in North Africa, it was no wonder that Rommel himself fell ill. For some time his medical adviser in North Africa, Professor Horster, had been urging his patient to return to Europe for rest and treatment. Horster had diagnosed Rommel as suffering from high blood pressure, as well as problems with his blood circulation and liver. Recently Rommel had shown signs of feeling faint and Horster had ordered him to remain in bed.

On 26 August Lieutenant Alfred Berndt wrote to Rommel's wife:

> *Dear Frau Rommel. The reason for my letter is to inform you about the state of the Marshal's health. Your husband has now been 19 months in Africa, which is longer than any other officer over 40 has stood so far, and, according to the doctors, an astonishing physical feat. All this has left its mark. In addition to all the symptoms of a heavy cold and the digestive disturbances typical*

*of Africa, he has recently shown signs of
exhaustion. The Fuehrer has been informed and
it has been agreed that he will receive a long
period of sick leave in Europe once the future of
this theatre has been decided. Until that time we
will do everything we can to make his life easier
and persuade him to look after himself. I ask you,
Madam, not to worry. As for his personal safety,
I shall do everything possible to safeguard it, for
every one of us, officers and men, would be ready
to die for the Marshal.*

By 29 August, Rommel insisted that he had recovered
enough to begin preparations for his attack on the Allied
positions. Realizing that he needed to attack before mid-
September, and wanting the advantage of a full moon to
help in a night attack, Rommel had decided on the night of
30 August for his assault. However, he still had huge
supply problems. The ammunition and petrol promised to
him by Marshal Cavellero had still not arrived. The full
moon, which was vital to his operation, was already on
the wane.

Under pressure from Rommel, Cavallero assured him
that tankers would arrive under heavy escort in a matter
of hours, or at the latest, the next day. In the hope that this
promise would be fulfilled, but above all in the certainty
that if he did not act during this full moon his last chance
of an offensive would be gone for ever, Rommel gave the
order for the attack to begin on the night of 30–31 August.

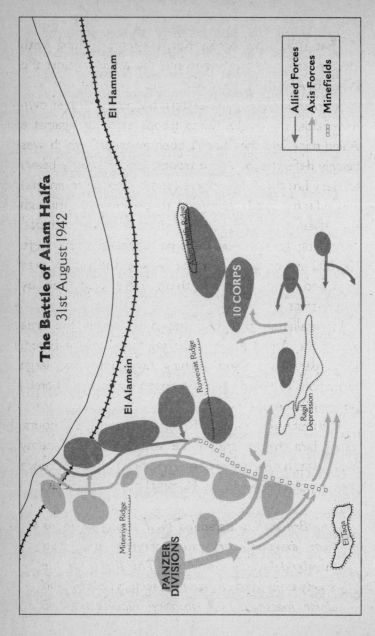

The Battle of Alam Halfa
31st August 1942

El Hammam

El Alamein

Alam Halfa Ridge

10 CORPS

Ruweisat Ridge

Ragil Depression

Miteiriya Ridge

PANZER DIVISIONS

El Taqa

Allied Forces
Axis Forces
Minefields

That night the Afrika Korps infantry, along with Panzer tank divisions, went into the attack against the Allied El Alamein front.

Soon after passing the eastern boundary of their own minefields, the Afrika Korps troops came up against a Allied minefield they hadn't been aware of, which was heavily defended by Allied troops. Under intense heavy artillery fire the Axis sappers (bomb-disposal engineers) and infantry finally managed to clear a way through the Allied minefields, although it took three attempts. According to the Afrika Korps' estimate there were 150,000 mines in the sector where the attack was launched, and many of them were protected by booby-traps.

In retaliation the RAF began to target the area where the Afrika Korps' attacking force was gathered. With parachute flares turning night into day, large formations of Allied aircraft dropped hundreds of bombs on the Axis troops.

The first report reached Rommel at about 0800 hours, telling him that owing to the strength of the enemy minefields, his Panzer divisions had been unable to reach their appointed objectives. Rommel noted in his diary:

The British had defended their strong positions with extraordinary stubbornness and had thereby delayed our advance. This had given the enemy units in the threatened sectors time to send alarm messages and situation reports back to

British HQ, and had enabled the British commander to take the necessary counter-measures. My plan for the motorized forces – to advance 30 miles east by moonlight and then strike at dawn – had not worked.

The element of surprise, the basis of Rommel's whole plan, had been lost. It was now impossible for him to continue with a wide sweep to the east, as his flanks would have been under constant threat from the Allies in the south and north. Instead, Rommel decided to turn to the north. The object of his attack was the Alam Halfa ridge, the same ridge that Montgomery had also identified as the key position at El Alamein. According to Luftwaffe air reconnaissance, this ridge was heavily defended by the Allies, and Rommel ordered the Luftwaffe to attack it.

Meanwhile, the vehicles and tanks of the Afrika Korps were painfully grinding their way through the soft sand. Driving sandstorms blew on and off all day, making the lives of the men a misery – although these sandstorms also prevented the RAF from making any heavy attacks on Rommel's forces.

Due to the tough going, the Afrika Korps tanks were using much more petrol than had been anticipated, and soon they began to run out. Because of this, at 1600 hours, Rommel called off the attack on the ridge. Worse was to come, however. Rommel noted in his journal:

Rommel, Commander of the Afrika Korps, and nicknamed the "Desert Fox", consults battle plans with his staff in 1941.

A British Crusader tank passes a burning German Panzer tank during November 1941.

German infantry encircle Allied troops at Mersa el Brega in Cyrenaica (the eastern side of Libya) in April 1942.

Allied sappers use mine-detectors to locate mines buried by the Afrika Korps.

German heavy artillery in action in January 1943.

Field Marshal Montgomery, Commander of the Allied 8th Army, welcomes Winston Churchill to Tripoli, Libya, in February 1943.

Two Indian gunners at their machine-gun in the Libyan desert, contributing their services to the Allied army.

Montgomery looks on as General Kinzel of the German army signs the surrender on 4 May 1945.

After nightfall our forces became the target for heavy RAF attacks. All movement was instantly pinned down by low-flying attacks. Soon many of our vehicles were alight and burning furiously.

By the end of August, the petrol that Rommel had been promised by Cavallero had still not arrived in Africa. His attempts to force a way through the Allied minefields were also being seriously hampered by firing from the Allied tanks and heavy artillery.

On 2 September Rommel drove through the area occupied by the Afrika Korps. Between ten and twelve o'clock this position was bombed no less than six times by Allied aircraft. Rommel wrote:

On one occasion I only just had time to throw myself into a slit trench before the bombs fell. A spade lying on the soil beside the trench was pierced clean through by an 8-inch splinter and the red-hot metal fragment fell beside me in the trench.

The Afrika Korps tried to launch another attack on the Allied front line during the afternoon, but the Allied tanks were now firmly established in their new positions, and once more Rommel's Panzer divisions were forced to retreat with heavy losses. Throughout the day RAF bombers relentlessly pounded the Germans and the Italians from the air.

That evening Rommel met Field Marshal Kesselring who was the representative of the German High Command in Africa. He asked Kesselring to use his planes to try and stop the RAF from carrying out their deadly attacks. Kesselring promised to do all he could, but that night the Afrika Korps once more suffered a non-stop pounding by powerful Allied bomber formations, without full protection by the Luftwaffe. A steady succession of parachute flares dropped by the bombers kept the whole of the desert bathed in a brilliant light to help them find their targets. Magnesium fire bombs, which were impossible to put out, lay on the ground lighting up the whole area. Meanwhile, vast quantities of bombs, even some land-mines, were dropped on to Rommel's troops. Many of his Afrika Korps' anti-aircraft guns were targeted by the Allies and destroyed. Hundreds of Afrika Korps vehicles were destroyed or damaged.

By now Rommel realized that his offensive no longer had any hope of succeeding. He decided to retreat to El Quattara. His hope was that Montgomery would follow him and he could launch a counter-attack against the Allies. However, Montgomery was not going to play the game the way that Rommel wanted him to. As the Afrika Korps began its withdrawal, the 8th Army remained firmly where it was. Montgomery was leaving no room for Rommel to make one of his famous surprise counter-attacks.

Rommel's frustration and disappointment is clear in his diary:

The impression we gained of the new British commander, General Montgomery, was that of a very cautious man who was not prepared to take any sort of risk... On the morning of 6 September we completed our withdrawal. With the failure of this offensive our last chance of gaining the Suez Canal has gone.

Montgomery
The Great Deception
31 August – 22 October 1942

AFTER THE BATTLE OF ALAM HALFA both sides settled into a period when they carried out repairs to their damaged equipment, sought fresh supplies, and took stock of the enemy while preparing their next moves. During this time the RAF, on Montgomery's orders, continued to attack the Afrika Korps supply lines.

Montgomery was well aware that, although his forces had held firm against the Afrika Korps attack at Alam Halfa, the defensive strategy he had adopted so far would not be enough to win the war in North Africa. Montgomery had promised to drive Rommel out, and the only way to do that was to launch his own attack against the Afrika Korps. But how was he going to do it? Rommel's forces had regrouped and now occupied a line running south from the coast to the Quattara Depression, a distance of about 45 miles. Rommel was also strengthening his defences, and these included deep and extensive minefields.

Montgomery's intended strategy was: first, to punch a hole in the enemy positions; second, to push the tanks and men of his 10th Corps through this hole into enemy territory; and third, to widen the attack from this breach in the enemy defences, and at the same time attack both flanks of the Afrika Korps positions.

When working out the exact date and time that he would launch his attack, Montgomery knew that a full moon was necessary. The main problem would be the minefields. The sappers, whose job was to disable the mines so that the tanks could move forward, had to be able to see what they were doing. A waning moon (the time immediately after a full moon, when the moonlight begins to dim) was not good enough. A waxing moon (the time immediately before a full moon, when the moon continues to brighten) was essential, because he knew it was likely the battle would last at least a week before his troops would be able to finally break out and get through the Afrika Korps lines. This limited his choice to one definite period each month.

Montgomery had promised the 8th Army that he would not launch his offensive until he was sure his troops were ready and all his supplies were in place. He knew he could not be ready for the September full moon and be sure of success. The next full moon after that would be on 24 October. Montgomery set the date for his major attack as the night of the 23 October. He sent a message to London giving his intended attack date. The Government responded by saying this was too long to wait. Field Marshal Alexander received a message from the prime minister saying that the attack must be in September. Churchill went on to say that this was to synchronize with planned Russian offensives that were going to take place in September against German troops on the Eastern Front in Europe.

London also wanted Montgomery's offensive to take place before Operation Torch (the Allied landings that were to take place early in November at the western side of North Africa). They believed that in this way Rommel would retreat during October and would be caught by the invading Allied forces coming from the west.

Montgomery insisted that his preparations could not be completed in time for a September offensive, and any attack made then would fail. If he could hold off for one month, he guaranteed complete success. He later wrote that:

If a September attack was ordered by Whitehall, they would have to get someone else to do it. Alexander backed me up whole heartedly, and the reply to London was sent on those lines. We heard no more about a September attack.

Montgomery was all too aware of Rommel's skill at out-thinking his opponents. Rommel was a clever military tactician and Montgomery knew he would be receiving detailed reports of all Allied movements. From these reports Rommel would be able to work out where the main thrust of the Allied attack would be aimed, and he would strengthen his defences at these points. So, Montgomery decided to defeat Rommel by cunning. In his memoirs, he writes:

I decided to plan for tactical surprise, and to conceal from the enemy the exact places where the blows would fall and the exact times. This would involve a great deception plan.

Although he claimed all the credit for the way this plan was carried out, Montgomery was assisted in his strategy by a British stage magician called Maskelyne. Maskelyne had been sent to join the forces in North Africa as an entertainer, and he was keen to use his skills as an illusionist to help the war effort. Magicians often use the technique of misdirection to divert their audience's attention away from the real trickery and Maskelyne was a master of this system. Using the illusionist's advice and experience, Montgomery's "great deception plan" had two aims. The first was to fool Rommel into thinking that the Allied attack was planned for November rather than October. The second was to mislead Rommel into thinking that Montgomery planned to launch the main thrust of his attack at the Afrika Korps lines towards the south, while in fact the real push was to go through the north.

As part of his deception, Montgomery used a variation of one of the tricks that Rommel had employed when he first arrived in Africa in 1940: dummy vehicles. In Montgomery's case, he used fake lorries and fake supply dumps to mislead the Afrika Korps into assuming that he was building up his transport and supplies at the southern end of his position at Alamein.

Montgomery carried out his plan in three stages:

1) During daylight hours, when Montgomery knew that German reconnaissance planes would be reporting on his movements, he sent hundreds of lorries, all loaded with vast amounts of ammunition and supplies, to the south of his position at Alamein.

2) When night fell, under the cover of darkness Montgomery moved most of these lorries, complete with their supplies and ammunition, back to the north. (Some remained in the south because the troops there would need them.) Once these lorries were back in the north, they were hidden under sand-coloured camouflage netting.

3) Meanwhile, in the south, during the night, imitation lorries were built – some made from wood, some from empty crates stacked up with cloth draped over them. Other empty crates were arranged to look like supply and ammunition dumps. When the German reconnaissance planes flew over the Allied positions the next day, they thought the fake lorries and supply and ammunition dumps were the real thing.

To add to this deception, Montgomery ordered

engineers to construct a dummy pipeline from the centre of his position towards the south, where his dummy equipment was stored. Every day they dug trenches leading southwards, into which they laid pipes, and then covered them with sand. The engineers were told to work at a pace that meant that if they were constructing a real pipeline, it would not be finished until the end of November. Montgomery depended on the Afrika Korps reconnaissance planes taking photographs of his position that would show all this activity.

As the finishing touch to his "great deception", Montgomery got his wireless operators to send signals between his divisions which, when intercepted by the Afrika Korps, suggested that the bulk of his tanks were moving to the southern end of his position.

Meanwhile, at the north of the Alamein position, Montgomery ordered the digging of slit trenches – narrow trenches in the ground that could be covered with sand-coloured sheeting. His plan was to hide the infantry soldiers in these trenches before the attack, so they would be invisible to German reconnaissance aircraft.

As with the Battle of Alam Halfa, the success of Montgomery's planned offensive depended heavily on the RAF. On the day before Montgomery intended the operation to start, the RAF was to carry out heavy attacks against the Afrika Korps airfields to prevent air reconnaissance by the enemy. Then, on 23 October at 2200 hours, the whole bomber effort was to be turn against the Afrika Korps artillery. Shortly before daylight on 24 October, the RAF and the forces on the ground were to co-ordinate their actions for a full- frontal attack on the Afrika Korps positions.

Montgomery wanted every soldier in his army to be mentally prepared for the battle that lay ahead. In his journal he noted:

> *Morale is the biggest thing in war. We must raise the morale of our soldiery to the highest pitch: they must be made enthusiastic. There must be no weak links in our mental fitness.*

However, he knew that the soldiers would not stand up to the stress and strain of battle unless they were also physically fit. He was aware that the impending action might go on for many days and the outcome could well depend on which side could stand up to the continuous strain of hard fighting. He was not convinced that the soldiers under his command were really as tough as they looked:

> *They are sunburnt and brown, but they seldom move anywhere on foot and they have led a static life for many weeks. During the next month it is essential to make our officers and men really fit. Ordinary fitness is not enough, they must be tough and hard.*

Montgomery introduced a training programme that was more intensive than many of the men had experienced before. It was the same policy he had brought in when he had been commanding the defence forces on the south coast in England two years earlier. Every day the men exercised: they completed obstacle courses, lifted weights, and ran carrying heavy objects such as rocks and crates, as well as undertaking various other exercises aimed at increasing their physical fitness.

Montgomery also demanded that the Officers commanding the men were equally tough, both physically and mentally. He had been especially annoyed at the large number of Allied prisoners-of-war who had surrendered when attacked in earlier campaigns and wanted to ensure his own men would stand firm. He complained in his diary:

There have been far too many unwounded prisoners taken in this war. We must impress on our officers, NCOs and men that when they are cut off or surrounded, and there appears to be no hope of survival, they must organise themselves into a defensive locality [using whatever is available to make defensive walls] and hold out where they are. Nothing is ever hopeless so long as troops have stout hearts and have weapons and ammunition.

No man would be allowed to surrender. Every man would stand and fight. This was a battle that Montgomery intended to win.

Rommel
The Dogs of War
7 September – 22 October 1942

THROUGHOUT OCTOBER 1942, the RAF continued to bomb the Afrika Korps supply ships sailing across the Mediterranean from Italy to North Africa, bringing the petrol and ammunition that Rommel needed so desperately.[3] The RAF also kept up a constant heavy bombing of the North African ports, so that even those supply ships that did reach the Libyan coast had difficulty in being unloaded.

Rommel's forces were reaching the end of the stocks they had captured and lack of food and petrol was becoming a serious problem. The numbers of soldiers reporting ill as a result of bad or inadequate food were particularly high in divisions that had been a long time in Africa, and among troops who had not been tested for

3 The ships carrying petrol, that Marshal Cavallero had promised Rommel would reach him in time for his offensive at the end of August, in fact didn't arrive in North Africa until 8 September, too late to help Rommel with his attack.

their fitness to serve in tropical climates. The desert was beginning to take its toll.

Rommel's own health was still causing concern. On 9 September he wrote to his wife:

Dearest Lu. My health is now fairly well restored. However, the doctor is pressing me hard to have a break in Germany and doesn't want me to postpone it any longer.

Convinced from the reports he received from the air reconnaissance that Montgomery would not launch his attack until late November, Rommel bowed to pressure from his medical advisers and decided to go to Germany for the six-week medical treatment that had been planned for him.

On 22 September General Stumme arrived in North Africa to take over command of the Panzer army, while Rommel returned to Germany on sick leave. However, Rommel told Stumme that if Montgomery launched his attack earlier than was expected, then he intended to cut short his treatment and return to North Africa to resume command of the Afrika Korps.

Rommel then flew from North Africa to Italy, where he met Mussolini on 24 September. Rommel warned the Italian leader that the supply situation in North Africa was worsening. Without more supplies he believed the Afrika Korps simply couldn't funtion and might as well pull out of North Africa. Despite the sympathy

Mussolini expressed for Rommel's position, the German Commander came away from the meeting convinced that Mussolini did not believe a word he had said.

Immediately afterwards, Rommel flew to Berlin and reported to Adolf Hitler and Hermann Goering (the Commander-in-Chief of the Luftwaffe and Hitler's second in command). Rommel reported his failure at Alam Halfa, and said the cause of it was *"the tremendous superiority of the British in the air"*. He also insisted that the German troops in North Africa must receive a fair allocation of ammunition and petrol. He pointed out that the number of Germans fighting in North Africa was double the number of Italian soldiers, yet they were receiving a much smaller amount of supplies.

During the meeting Goering tried to claim that Rommel was exaggerating the difficulties he was facing in North Africa. When Rommel told them that Allied fighter-bombers had destroyed his tanks with American 40-mm shells, Goering sneered back at Rommel, *"That's completely impossible. The Americans only know how to make razor blades."* Struggling to maintain his self-control, Rommel replied: *"We could do with some of those razor blades, Herr Reichsmarschall."*

To back up his argument, Rommel had brought with him a solid armour-piercing shell that had been fired at one of his tanks by a low-flying Allied aircraft. It had killed almost the entire tank crew. Rommel showed this shell to Hitler and Goering as proof of the strength of artillery his men were facing.

The Dogs of War

Goering fell angrily silent at this, and Hitler promised Rommel that supplies to the Afrika Korps would be considerably increased during the next few weeks. German weapons manufacturers had agreed to deliver the huge number of tanks and ammunition Hitler demanded. However, what Hitler didn't know was that the numbers he demanded were impossible to produce in the time. People who openly disagreed with Hitler often suffered tragic repercussions in Nazi Germany, and so the manufacturers kept the truth from him.

Back home in Germany, Rommel was forced to face the German press. With pressure on him from politicians to give a positive viewpoint, he knew he could not offer a true account of how bad things were in Africa. Rommel hoped that if he led people to believe that the Afrika Korps defences were very strong, perhaps the Allies would postpone their forthcoming attack. So Rommel told the German news reporters that everything was going well in North Africa, and that victory was near.

After this, Rommel went to Semmering, a mountain resort in Austria near Vienna, to receive treatment for his liver and blood-pressure conditions. The news that filtered through to him from North Africa did not help his recovery, however. Attacks by the Allied air force were increasing, and the 8th Army appeared to be growing steadily stronger. The Afrika Korps lived in constant expectation of a major Allied attack. General Stumme now believed that the attack would be launched at several points simultaneously, but all his intelligence reports suggested that it would mainly take place in the south. According to German estimates from his HQ in North Africa, the Allies had a two-to-one superiority in tanks.

Rommel realized that he had to prevent the Allies from breaking through the Afrika Korps lines at all costs. Issuing orders from Austria, Rommel arranged the construction of a strong defence system right along the Afrika Korps front line, with a mobile force of reserve troops and tanks at the rear. Rommel hoped that a really strong defensive front line would be able to hold out against even the heaviest Allied attack long enough for these mobile reserve forces to come up and join the defences wherever they were needed.

The Afrika Korps defences were laid out so that the minefields in front of their positions were held by light outposts only, each manned by just a small force of men. The main defences were located a mile behind the most forward minefield. The tanks of the Panzer divisions were positioned behind this main first defence line so that their guns could fire into the area in front of the line, and increase the defensive fire-power of that sector.

About half a million landmines were used in the construction of the Afrika Korps defensive minefields, including captured Allied mines. Huge numbers of captured Allied bombs and shells were also built into the

Afrika Korps defence. The majority of the mines laid were anti-tank mines, but many thousands were Afrika Korps anti-personnel "S" mines. These were set in the forward areas against Allied infantry attacks. They were operated by a trip wire, or sometimes by remote control. When they were triggered they threw a bomb to waist height. When this bomb exploded it hurled hundreds of deadly ball-bearings in all directions.

The Afrika Korps outposts were also provided with guard dogs, who would bark and raise the alarm if there were any secret Allied approaches to the minefields under cover of darkness.

With Montgomery preparing his offensive, and Rommel desperate to get back to North Africa and take control the stage was set for a major confrontation between the two armies.

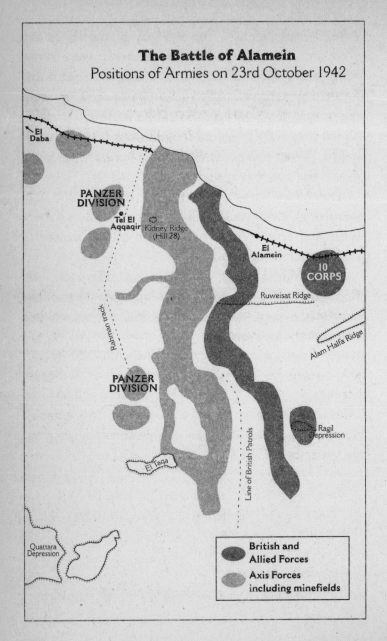

The Battle of Alamein
Positions of Armies on 23rd October 1942

El Daba

PANZER DIVISION

Tel El Aqqaqir

Kidney Ridge (Hill 28)

El Alamein

10 CORPS

Rahman track

Ruweisat Ridge

Alam Halfa Ridge

PANZER DIVISION

Ragil Depression

El Taqa

Line of British Patrols

Quattara Depression

British and Allied Forces

Axis Forces including minefields

Mines and Bayonets

23 – 24 October 1942

MONTGOMERY'S PLAN WAS to attack in three stages. The first would consist of a heavy barrage of shelling on the enemy positions beginning at 2140 hours, followed by an infantry advance at 2200 hours. Then, at 0200 hours, tanks would be unleashed against the Afrika Korps defences.

On 23 October 1942, the day of the attack, Montgomery issued the following personal message to every member of the 8th Army:

> WHEN I ASSUMED COMMAND OF THE EIGHTH ARMY
> I SAID THAT THE MANDATE WAS TO DESTROY
> ROMMEL AND HIS ARMY, AND THAT IT WOULD BE
> DONE AS SOON AS WE WERE READY.
> WE ARE READY NOW.
> THE BATTLE WHICH IS NOW ABOUT TO BEGIN WILL

BE ONE OF THE DECISIVE BATTLES OF HISTORY. IT WILL BE THE TURNING POINT OF THE WAR. THE EYES OF THE WHOLE WORLD WILL BE ON US, WATCHING ANXIOUSLY WHICH WAY THE BATTLE WILL SWING. WE CAN GIVE THEM THEIR ANSWER AT ONCE: "IT WILL SWING OUR WAY."

WE HAVE FIRST-CLASS EQUIPMENT: GOOD TANKS; GOOD ANTI-TANK GUNS; PLENTY OF ARTILLERY AND PLENTY OF AMMUNITION; AND WE ARE BACKED BY THE FINEST AIR STRIKING FORCE IN THE WORLD.

ALL THAT IS NECESSARY IS THAT EACH ONE OF US, EVERY OFFICER AND MAN, SHOULD ENTER THIS BATTLE WITH THE DETERMINATION TO SEE IT THROUGH — TO FIGHT AND TO KILL — AND FINALLY, TO WIN.

IF WE DO ALL THIS THERE CAN BE ONLY ONE RESULT — TOGETHER WE WILL HIT THE ENEMY FOR SIX, RIGHT OUT OF NORTH AFRICA.

THE SOONER WE WIN THIS BATTLE, WHICH WILL BE THE TURNING POINT OF THIS WAR, THE SOONER WE SHALL ALL GET BACK HOME TO OUR FAMILIES.

THEREFORE, LET EVERY OFFICER AND MAN ENTER THE BATTLE WITH A STOUT HEART, AND WITH THE DETERMINATION TO DO HIS DUTY SO LONG AS HE HAS BREATH IN HIS BODY.

AND LET NO MAN SURRENDER SO LONG AS HE IS UNWOUNDED, AND CAN FIGHT.

LET US ALL PRAY THAT THE LORD MIGHTY IN BATTLE WILL GIVE US THE VICTORY."

Astonishingly, Montgomery would take no part in the opening of the actual battle. As we have already seen, Montgomery always insisted on getting a proper night's sleep, and the night of 23 October was going to be no different as far as he was concerned. Whether this showed enormous confidence in his own planning, or even greater confidence in the Generals under his command, the fact is that he recorded in his journal for that fateful night:

> In the evening I read a book and went to bed early. At 9.40 p.m. the barrage of over one thousand guns opened, and the Eighth Army went into the attack. At that moment I was asleep in my caravan. There was nothing I could do and I knew I would be needed later.

But for the front-line Allied troops, there was no chance of sleep. For the sappers, in particular, the prospect of what lay ahead of them must have been terrifying. Many of them were just young men, in their late teens or early twenties. Earlier in the day they had been told by a senior Officer, in frank terms, what they could expect:

> I have to give it you straight: right behind you will be a whole division relying on you sappers to open the lanes for the tanks and infantry to pass through. Also behind you will be a thousand guns. They will put up a terrific barrage as you sappers go in. Some of you will be killed, or lose

an arm or leg, because Jerry will be trying to stop you. There will be mortaring, Stuka dive bombing and the rest.

Before the battle, the sappers had been put into slit trenches right at the very front line. The only protection they wore against enemy gunfire was a steel helmet; their only weapon was a rifle, with a bayonet. The bayonet was to be used to probe the ground in front of them for the deadly mines.

As the heavy artillery opened up on the Afrika Korps positions, each young man knew he had just 20 minutes left until he had to get out of the trench and walk towards the enemy gunfire, into the minefield.

For those 20 minutes the heavy guns of the Allies pounded the Afrika Korps positions, and then, at 2200 hours, the sappers were sent out from their trenches to advance into the minefields, the infantry divisions following behind them. All the time the Afrika Korps poured gunfire into them, but still they moved forward. One observer from an armoured unit said later:

The sight of sappers lining up and going over the ridge to probe for mines with bayonets was terrible and awe-inspiring to watch. Every one of them deserved a medal as they seemed to go to a certain death. They no sooner went over than bursts of enemy machine-gun seemed to wipe them out; then another line would form up and move over the top.

Under any circumstances, the job of finding and disabling mines could be deadly. At night, under a hail of enemy gunfire, it was almost suicidal. Sapper Easthope of 577th Field Company recalled:

> *We used bayonets to find the mines. You probed lightly – if you struck something solid you explored gently around it with your hands. If you find a wire, where did it lead? Don't cut it, don't lift it. Expose it and find out where it goes. You had to take your chances when clearing mines. One chap from an S mine got a pellet in the jaw which came out by his neck behind the ear.*

The infantrymen were no better protected against enemy gunfire. They were dressed in shorts and wore steel helmets. Many wore cardigans against the cold of the desert night. In addition to his rifle and bayonet, every infantryman's equipment included two grenades, a bandolier (a long ammunition belt hung from around the neck) containing 50 rounds of extra ammunition. He also carried one day's rations, a full water-bottle, a pick and shovel, a groundsheet, and he had four sandbags tied to his pack. (If the ground was too hard for him to use his pick and shovel to dig a defensive position; he could make a low defensive wall with the sandbags.) Each man carried enough supplies to fight for at least 24 hours.

To help the advancing troops, searchlights illuminated the night sky above the minefields. However, they also exposed them to the enemy guns. It was vital that the Allied heavy artillery kept the Afrika Korps guns bombarded if the sappers and infantry were to be protected.

Because of the horrendous conditions the sappers were working under, not all minefield clearances were successful. For one thing, the enemy mines had been scattered at random across the minefields, so to find them all meant close scrutiny of every step taken – not an easy task when surrounded by shellfire, gunfire, smoke and deafening noise. Some mine-clearing was carried out by "Scorpions" or "flail tanks" that had been especially adapted to deal with mines. A rotating drum with heavy chains on it had been fitted at the front of each tank. As it moved forward, the drum rotated, and the heavy chains hit the ground, setting off any mines it struck. However, sometimes mines were missed by one tank and detonated by the next one to go over them, blocking the route for those coming behind.

The infantrymen of the Scottish Highland Regiments, as was their long tradition, went into battle to the sound of their pipers playing the bagpipes. Captain Grant Murray of 5th Seaforth Highlanders remembered the start of the attack:

> *The hands of my watch seemed to creep round as we lay listening and watching. To our front all was quiet apart from some machine-gun fire. As zero hour drew near I twisted round and*

looked back towards our own lines. Suddenly the whole horizon went pink and for a second or two there was still perfect silence, and then the noise of the Eighth Army's guns hit us in a solid wall of sound that made the whole earth shake. Through the din we made out other sounds – the whine of shells overhead, the clatter of machine guns and, eventually, the sound of the bagpipes. Then we saw a sight that will live forever in our memories – line upon line of steel-helmeted figures with rifles at the high port, bayonets catching in the moonlight, and over all the wailing of the bagpipes. As they passed they gave us the thumbs-up sign, and we watched them plod on towards the enemy lines, which by this time were shrouded in smoke. Our final sight of them was just as they entered the smoke, with the enemy's defensive fire falling among them.

The Afrika Korps' defensive fire took a terrible toll on the Scottish Highlanders. One brigade of the Black Watch regiment advanced through a field of anti-personnel mines against enemy fire; by the time they reached their objective only one Officer was left standing. Another Black Watch company met fierce mortar and artillery fire nearer the enemy lines, taking heavy casualties, including 5 Officers killed and 10 wounded; 65 men killed and 135 wounded.

At 0200 hours, the Allied tanks moved forward to Miteiriya Ridge, where they ran into enemy artillery and anti-tank gunfire. They stayed behind the ridge and fired at the enemy from long range. The German Panzer divisions launched a series of counter-attacks against the Allied tanks behind the ridge, but they were beaten off and took heavy losses.

Meanwhile, to the south, an operation was mounted by two Allied tank divisions with the aim of forcing two gaps in the minefields north of Himeimat. At the same time a brigade of Fighting French soldiers attacked the Afrika Korps lines, but were held up after they hit a series of mines scattered between the two major minefields. The French pressed on and took their objective, but soft sand delayed their supporting vehicles and they were driven back by a counter-attack delivered by an Afrika Korps armoured column.

When Montgomery woke just before dawn the next morning he received reports from de Guingand about the night's battle:

> *Situation on 24 October. In the north we had successfully broken into the enemy positions and secured a good bridgehead [a way forward into the Afrika Korps front lines]. But attempts to pass the armour straight through and into the open and to the west of the Afrika Korps defensive system had been unsuccessful.*

Rommel

The Battle of Alamein

23 – 24 October 1942

WHEN THE BATTLE OF ALAMEIN began on the night of 23 October 1942, Rommel was still in Germany receiving medical treatment, and Montgomery was in bed, fast asleep. It must surely be one of those rare times in military history when a major battle begins without either of the two opposing Commanders being actively involved.

For the Afrika Korps, the day of 23 October had passed just like any other day on the Alamein front, until 2140 hours that night when an artillery barrage of huge proportions opened over their whole position. Such an assault of shells and bombing by the RAF had never before been seen in North Africa. It was in the northern sector of the Afrika Korps positions that the assault was most intense. The accuracy with which the Allies bombarded them was devastating to the Axis troops and they suffered enormous casualties.

The Afrika Korps communications network was smashed by this onslaught, and reports from the front to their HQ – situated on the coast only a few miles behind the battle front – virtually ceased. The soldiers at the outposts at the front fought to the last round of ammunition, and then either surrendered or were killed.

By 0100 hours the advancing Allied infantry, with tank support, had overrun the Afrika Korps outposts and penetrated the main defence line over a width of six miles. The Afrika Korps infantry resisted as hard as they could, but most of their heavy guns had been smashed by the enemy artillery fire. Again and again the Allies brought up tanks to attack the front lines.

Back in the Afrika Korps HQ, General Stumme knew that his stock of ammunition was running desperately low, and he refused to authorize his artillery to open fire on the Allied positions. Writing much later, Rommel said:

> *This was a mistake, in my view, for it would have at least reduced the weight of the British attack. When the artillery did finally open fire it was unable to have anything like the effect it might have had earlier, for the British had by that time been able to install themselves in defence posts they had captured during the night.*

When dawn broke on 24 October, Afrika Korps HQ had still only received a few reports, and there was a lot of confusion about the situation at the front. To find out what was really going on, General Stumme decided to drive up there himself. The acting Chief of Staff, Colonel Westphal, urged the General to take an escort vehicle and signals truck with him as Rommel had always done. But Stumme refused to take any escort with him apart from his aide, Colonel Buechting, and their driver.

In the early hours of 24 October, heavy Allied artillery again opened up on the Afrika Korps positions, this time concentrated on the southern sector. Having overrun the Axis outposts the Allied advance was brought to a halt in front of the main defensive line. That afternoon Rommel received a telephone call at the Semmering from Field Marshal Keitel. Keitel told him that the Allies had been attacking at Alamein with powerful artillery and bomber support since the previous evening and that General Stumme was missing. Keitel asked whether Rommel would be well enough to return to Africa and resume command. Rommel said that he would.

He was now desperate to return to Africa, and salvage the situation. He later remembered:

I spent the next few hours in a state of acute anxiety, until the evening when I received a telephone call from Hitler himself. He said that Stumme was still missing – either captured or killed – and asked whether I could start for Africa immediately...

Rommel ordered his aircraft and left for Africa at 0700 hours the next morning.

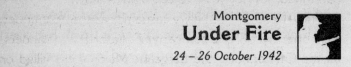

Montgomery
Under Fire
24 – 26 October 1942

AT 1500 HOURS ON 24 OCTOBER the Allied attack on the Afrika Korps front line at the north of their position started again. Montgomery sent his tank divisions out to push through the enemy lines, and by 1800 hours they had made their way through the western minefields and reached a position at one side of the Afrika Korps defences.

Montgomery's forces at the southern end of the Alamein position had the hardest task, because of Montgomery's "great deception plan", which had led to most of the Afrika Korps defensive forces being massed in this area. However, one division, acting on Montgomery's *must and will get forward* instructions, attacked again, and this time managed to open up a small gap in the Afrika Korps defences. A light armoured brigade pushed forward through this gap but they came up against scattered mines and anti-tank gunfire, and it was obvious they would suffer heavy casualties if they continued, so they were forced to withdraw.

The Allies suffered heavy casualties as they continued their offensive. In one company of Seaforth Highlanders, all the Officers and the Sergeant Major were killed or wounded during their attack. However, this company did manage to reach their objective, led by the Company Clerk.

During 25 October, the German Panzer division made a series of counter-attacks, but the Allied tank divisions managed to fend off these attacks and cause heavy casualties to the Afrika Korps. Meanwhile, the Allied sappers were working to clear as many 16-yard gaps as possible through the minefields in order to speed up the progress of the tanks. At one gap the tanks of the Sherwood Rangers were waiting to go through, lined up nose-to-tail, along with their supply transport vehicles, when German aircraft came over and dropped bombs on their position. Twenty-five of the lorries were carrying petrol and ammunition and were soon ablaze. The Afrika Korps artillery used this huge fire as a target and began shelling the whole area, destroying tanks and vehicles, and killing and wounding the men.

Because of the intensity of the enemy machine-gun fire the sappers weren't able to mark the sides of the paths they had cleared with lengths of wire fencing, which was the usual practice. As a result, some of the tanks that followed the sappers through the gap misjudged its sides and hit mines. This disabled them and made them sitting targets for the enemy's heavy guns.

It became clear to Montgomery that any further advance against the Afrika Korps in the south was going to be very dangerous. At midday on 25 October he decided to stop that offensive and instead switch his main attack back to the north, with the aim of destroying the Axis forces along the coast.

In altering the main direction of his attack so quickly he hoped to surprise the enemy and take them unawares. He guessed that the Afrika Korps would be concentrating their defences against the New Zealand troops that were heading south, and would not be expecting this sudden attack to the north. He was right. An attack in the north by Australian divisions on the night of 25–26 October was completely successful as far as Montgomery was concerned: the Afrika Korps suffered some 300 casualties.

On 26 October, the Allies advanced about 1,000 yards as they pushed towards Miteiriya Ridge. That same night, an Allied motor brigade finally made it to Kidney Ridge.

Despite all the attacks that had been launched, it was with a mounting sense of frustration that Montgomery assessed the situation. With a series of carefully co-ordinated attacks on narrow fronts, his own infantry divisions had inflicted a heavy toll on the Afrika Korps infantry. However, his assault divisions had suffered serious casualties and the momentum of the Allied attack was diminishing.

The area in which Montgomery intended to carry out his major break-out through the enemy lines was still protected by lines of Afrika Korps anti-tank defences, and attempts to break through them had been unsuccessful.

The casualty figures for the 8th Army by the end of 26 October had reached 6,000. The Scottish Highland divisions had suffered some of the severest casualties, with 2,100 killed or wounded. And, despite these losses and the courage shown by the Allied troops in executing out this huge offensive, the 8th Army had still not broken through the Afrika Korps lines.

"Rivers of Blood"

25 – 28 October 1942

ROMMEL REACHED HIS HEADQUARTERS in North Africa at dusk on 25 October and learnt that General Stumme's body had been found at midday. It appeared that Stumme was being driven to the battlefield along a track when his car had suddenly been fired on by Allied anti-tank machine-guns. The driver of the car had immediately swung the car round and General Stumme had leapt out and hung on to the outside of it, while the driver drove at top speed out of the enemy line of fire. It appeared that Stumme had suffered a heart attack and fallen off the car. (He had been known to suffer from high blood pressure and had not really been fit for tropical service.)

Reports received by Rommel that evening informed him that the Allies had taken possession of part of the German defensive minefield. The continuing petrol shortage made any major movement on the part of the Afrika Korps impossible and allowed for only short-distance counter-attacks to defend the most vulnerable points along their lines.

Units of the Panzer division had launched counter-attacks several times on 24 and 25 October, but they had suffered terrible losses under the heavy fire of the Allied artillery and the RAF bombing attacks. By the evening of 25 October, only 31 out of the Panzer Division's 119 tanks remained serviceable. Rommel wrote in his journal:

> *That night our line again came under a heavy artillery barrage which soon developed into one long roll of fire. I slept only a few hours and was back on my command vehicle at 0500 hours [26 October], where I learnt that the British had spent the whole night assaulting our front under cover of their artillery, which in some places had fired as many as five hundred rounds for every one of ours.*

Shortly before midnight the Allies had succeeded in taking a point that Rommel had marked as "Hill 28" in the northern sector. (It was referred to by Montgomery as "Kidney Ridge".) Rommel ordered attacks to be launched on Hill 28, to be backed up by concentrated fire from the front-line German artillery and anti-aircraft units. But the Allies resisted determinedly and the

Germans gained ground very slowly. Sick at the slaughter of his men, Rommel wrote:

> *Rivers of blood were poured out over miserable strips of land which, in normal times, not even the poorest Arab would have bothered his head about.*

On 26th October Rommel went to the front to watch the attack by his forces, and saw his tanks bombarded mercilessly as load after load of bombs poured down from the Allied planes. Rommel gave orders to his artillery to try to break up the Allied forces north-east of Hill 28 by concentrated fire, but his gunners had too little ammunition to do it successfully.

Late in the afternoon, Afrika Korps dive-bomber formations made an attempt to break up the Allied lorry columns moving towards the north-west. However, about 60 Allied fighter planes counter-attacked the slower-moving Afrika Korps planes. The Italian pilots, desperate to lighten their loads and get away, dropped their bombs over their own lines, killing many of their own soldiers. The German pilots continued with their attack, but suffered heavy losses as a result of RAF fighter planes and Allied anti-aircraft fire.

Allied forces, supported by tanks, tried again and again to break out to the west through the German line south of Hill 28. Finally, in the afternoon, a thrust by

160 Allied tanks succeeded in wiping out an already severely damaged Italian battalion and pushed into the German line towards the south-west. Fierce fighting followed, in which the remaining Afrika Korps tanks managed to force the Allies back. But Rommel knew this was only a temporary relief.

In the evening of 26 October, Rommel's Italian forces managed to occupy the eastern and western edges of Hill 28, but the hill itself remained in Allied hands.

The supply situation for the Afrika Korps was now approaching disaster. Word arrived that the Italian tanker *Proserpina*, which Rommel had hoped would bring some relief to the petrol situation, had been bombed and sunk outside Tobruk. There was only enough petrol left to keep Rommel's supply vehicles between Tripoli and the front going for another two or three days.

Rommel decided to take a major gamble and send a German Panzer division and an Italian tank division to defend his position in the north. He was well aware that the petrol shortage would not allow these tanks to return south.

During the night of 26 October relays of Allied bombers continued their attack on the German positions, and at about 0200 hours the following morning an enormous Allied barrage of heavy guns suddenly began in the northern sector. Rommel reported that:

It was impossible to distinguish between gun-fire and exploding shells and the sky grew bright with the glare of muzzle-flashes and shell-bursts.

Continuous bombing attacks by the RAF seriously delayed the drive north by the Afrika Korps tank divisions.

By the morning of 27 October Rommel knew there was very little he could do except try to defend against further Allied attacks. He gave orders that all his units were to dig in and pin down the Allied assault forces during their approach with all-out fire from every gun they could bring to bear.

On 28 October some of Rommel's troops made a prolonged reconnaissance of Hill 28, searching for soft spots in the Allied front line. Two German Panzer divisions waited in the rear, ready to move forward if any weaknesses were found, but the RAF attacked these Panzer divisions so heavily that the lines of German tanks were scattered. With a sense of despair, Rommel realized that the German position was crumbling.

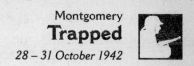

MONTGOMERY WAS BEGINNING to feel frustrated and trapped in his position at Alamein. All his attempts to break completely through the enemy positions and out the other side had failed. Partly this was because Montgomery refused to launch an all-out attack unless he was absolutely confident it would succeed. Against a master military strategist like Rommel, he could not afford to send his forces deep into the enemy's position where there was a chance they might be trapped and destroyed. He knew that if that happened, Rommel would launch his own counter-attack through the gap that was exposed. Montgomery had tried to find a weak link in Rommel's defences, and so far there was no evidence of one.

At this stage, Montgomery and Rommel were like two chess masters, each warily eyeing up the other's moves, each waiting for his opponent to make a mistake so that the decisive strike could be made. Eventually, Montgomery decided it was up to him to force Rommel to make a move, one that might expose a weakness in the Afrika Korps lines.

On the night of 28–29 October, Montgomery gave orders for an Australian division to launch a heavy attack northwards. They made good progress – about 200 prisoners were taken and a narrow wedge was driven into the enemy's positions. During 29 October and again early on 30 October, repeated counter-attacks by Afrika Korps tanks and infantry were thrown against the Australians in this wedge, but they managed to hold on to the ground they had won.

During the morning of 29 October, Montgomery learnt that some German divisions had moved up from the south into an area to the west of his position. Montgomery realized that Rommel had sent these divisions to support the Afrika Korps troops in the north.

Montgomery had, in fact, been intending to launch an attack towards the west, but now he changed his plans and decided instead to launch an attack towards the south. Rommel had now left much of the southern sector under the defences of the Italians, and Montgomery felt they might prove an easier target.

Montgomery ordered another Australian division to head northwards towards the coast on the night of 30–31 October. He hoped this move would confirm Rommel's fear about an Allied attack coming in the extreme north, and would also be a decoy move ahead of his attack in the south.

The Australians managed to cross the coast road and push forward to the sea, they then turned eastwards. With this action they trapped a whole German division. Rommel's other divisions launched a series of furious counter-attacks in an attempt to free their comrades. Towards evening some German tanks from the west managed to break through the Allied lines and join up with the trapped division. Finally the majority of the Germans fought their way out, but they suffered severe casualties.

Despite these continuing skirmishes along the front line neither side made any real progress. Montgomery was concerned that the two sides might end up in a stalemate. He knew that Operation Torch would soon be taking place, with British and American troops landing in West Africa. For that operation to succeed, Rommel's forces had to be destroyed, or forced into a major retreat across North Africa. So far there was still no sign of that happening. Sooner or later Montgomery knew he would have to make a hard and determined push to break out through the German lines.

Rommel
"The Battle is Raging"
28 – 31 October 1942

THE DEEP DESPAIR THAT Rommel felt at this time, as his army was collapsing around him, is shown in a letter to his wife, Lucie:

> *28 October 1942.*
> *Dearest Lu. Who knows whether I'll have a chance to sit down and write in peace in the next few days or ever again. Today there's still a chance. The battle is raging. Perhaps we will manage to be able to stick it out, in spite of all that's against us – but it may go wrong, and that would have very grave consequences for the whole course of the war, for North Africa would then fall to the British in a few days. We will do all we can. But the enemy's superiority is terrific and our resources small.*

Whether I would survive a defeat lies in God's hands. The lot of the vanquished is heavy. I'm happy in my own conscience that I've done all I can for victory and have not spared myself.
I realized so well in the few short weeks I was at home what you two [Lucie and their son, Manfred] mean to me. My last thought is of you.

By 28 October, the supply situation was disastrous for the Afrika Korps. From the Italian coast, more supply ships were being put to sea in order to fill the Afrika Korps' urgent need for ammunition and petrol. Unfortunately for Rommel, only a few of the supply ships he had been promised were going to Tobruk; most were bound for Benghazi, a port that was considered safer but that was much further away from the Afrika Korps front line. Transport, even from Tobruk, would take several days, and there was little hope of these supplies reaching Rommel's forces before it was too late.

Despite being short of fuel and ammunition, Rommel was determined to put up as much resistance as he could. In his memoirs for 28 October he wrote:

Because of the heavy casualties which had been suffered by the German-Italian infantry divisions, the whole of the Afrika Korps had to be put into the front line. I informed all commanders that this was a battle for life or death and that every officer and man had to give of his best.

At about 2100 hours on 28 October, a tremendous Allied barrage started to pound the area west of Hill 28. At 2200 hours, Montgomery launched a major assault. However, by concentrating every gun in the area against the advancing troops, Rommel's forces managed to break up the Allied attack. Farther to the north Allied tanks and infantry navigated the minefields and reached the Afrika Korps front line. For six hours the battle raged with tremendous fury, until finally the Afrika Korps front-line regiments were overrun by the Allied troops.

Rommel's deep distress is expressed in his diary:

> *No one can conceive the extent of my anxiety during this period. That night I hardly slept and by 0300 hours on 29 October, I was pacing up and down and turning over in my mind the likely course of the battle and the decisions I have to take.*

On 29 October he wrote to his wife:

> *Dearest Lu. The situation continues very grave. By the time this letter arrives, it will no doubt have been decided whether we can hold on or not. I haven't much hope left.*

The next day, 30 October, Rommel took stock of his situation. His army had been so badly battered that he could not now hope to stand up for long to the Allied breakthrough attempt, which was expected daily, even hourly. The only thing for him to do was to try to smuggle his infantry out under cover of darkness and hope to beat a fighting retreat to the west.

His withdrawal was just starting when a violent barrage of Allied shellfire targetted the sector held by Rommel's infantry in the north. Rommel's anti-aircraft artillery immediately responded, but were unable to break up the heavy concentration of Allied infantry and armoured guns in that sector. After an hour of continuous fire, the Australians launched an attack, pinning down a German regiment. At the same time a strong force of Allied tanks rolled in from the area north of Hill 28 and overran a battalion of Italians.

A further assault by the Allies led to a German infantry regiment being cut off from Rommel's main force. Rather than continue with his planned fighting retreat and leave these men to their fate, Rommel decided to launch a counter-attack against the forces surrounding the trapped regiment to try and rescue his men.

The counter-attack began at 1200 hours on 31 October. At first it failed to get through to their trapped comrades, as the Allies scattered the German tanks and infantry with concentrated artillery fire and air attacks. However, Rommel's forces kept attacking, and at last a sudden strike by the Germans succeeded in pushing the Allies back across the railway line to the south. Rommel's infantry regiment had been rescued, but his forces had taken a heavy beating as a result.

With his army almost in ruins, Rommel knew that retreat was his only option if his army was to survive.

Burning Lorries
2 – 4 November 1942

AT 0100 HOURS ON 2 NOVEMBER, Montgomery finally put his break-out attack, code named Operation Supercharge, into action.

The assaulting Allied troops at the front advanced behind a barrage of heavy fire from tanks and artillery. One thrust of this assault was carried out by a Maori battalion. The Maoris came under heavy fire soon after they launched their offensive, and their Colonel was wounded. They continued moving forward, fighting all the way. By dawn, the Maoris had reached their objective, capturing 162 Germans and 189 Italians at a loss of 33 men killed and 75 wounded. The advance by the Maoris had been a success and a new corridor through the enemy lines had been established.

As dawn broke the Allied armoured brigade ran into anti-tank gunfire so fierce that they suffered over 75 per cent casualties. Despite this they held on grimly to their position. Even after suffering such enormous losses, the armoured brigade managed to hold on to the bridgehead they had established into the enemy lines.

Two squadrons of Allied armoured cars had managed to get right out into the open desert as part of the forward thrust during the night. One of the squadron leaders gave the following account of their rapid advance against bewildered enemy opposition in the early hours before dawn, when it was still dark:

We left our location and passed through minefields in single file. No shot was fired at us. The enemy was too astounded to do anything as we came through, or else the Italian sections thought we were Germans and the German section thought we were Italians. They waved swastika flags at us with vigour and we replied with 'Achtung!' and anything else we could think of, which, with an answering wave, would get us through their lines. As it grew lighter they stared and blinked at us. Although a warning artillery barrage had been going on all night they couldn't believe their eyes. We passed within 10 yards of the muzzles of an entire battery of field artillery.

As the sun rose, the armoured cars passed a man in bed, in the open air. From the large number of vehicles and equipment surrounding him, they guessed that he was an Italian Quartermaster, and they threw a hand-grenade into one of the vehicles, destroying it and waking him up.

Picking their way through trenches and gun positions the Allied armoured car crews came upon what appeared to be a permanent headquarters. Lorries were dug in and men were asleep nearby. The Allied soldiers attacked the lorries with hand grenades and gunfire before the sleeping men could wake up and fight back. They destroyed 40 lorries by simply putting a bullet through the petrol tank of each and setting a match to the leak.

On 3 November, Montgomery recorded that

The Desert Air Force reported heavy traffic moving westwards on the coast road, but the enemy anti-tank gun screen held, and I Armoured Division was still unable to pierce it.

It was now clear to him that Rommel was getting ready for a withdrawal, but Montgomery knew his enemy would have great difficulty in getting his troops away owing to a shortage of transport and fuel. Montgomery expected that Rommel would try and hold the Allied forces off while he evacuated his troops, but as he recorded in his journal, *"I plan to complete the break out and get behind him."*

There was one thing Montgomery was sure of: he did not want Rommel and his army getting away. He had promised to destroy Rommel's army, and that was what he intended to do.

On the night of 3 – 4 November Montgomery launched a fast-moving thrust on a front of over four miles. Montgomery's intention was to break through the southern sector of the Afrika Korps anti-tank defences. Montgomery believed that if a gap could be made here, then the way would be clear for his forces to pass through the enemy lines and out into the open desert, outflanking the stronger German resistance to the north.

By the morning of 4 November the defensive German anti-tank guns had been forced back by the strength of Montgomery's attack, and a gap began to appear in the Afrika Korps lines. Into this gap Montgomery launched the full force of his armoured divisions. His big push forward had begun.

Alamein: "Victory or Death"

2 – 4 November 1942

BY DAWN ON 2 NOVEMBER, groups of Allied tanks and armoured cars had succeeded in breaking through the Axis lines and had began hunting down supply units. In the early hours, the Afrika Korps counter-attacked and achieved some success, although they lost many armoured vehicles, as their tanks were no match for the heavy Allied equivalents.

The Allies had now pushed more than two miles into the Axis lines. It was only by the desperate fire of all the available Afrika Korps artillery and anti-aircraft guns that a further Allied advance was prevented.

Rommel now sent more Panzer tanks to the front in a desperate attempt to try to stop the enemy wedge in his defences from widening. This led to violent confrontations between the opposing tanks. Throughout the battle Allied air force and artillery hammered away mercilessly at the

Axis troops. At midday, seven formations of Allied aircraft dropped hundreds of bombs on the enemy positions. With each raid, more of the Afrika Korps' big guns were put out of action.

In the early afternoon the dire situation in the north forced Rommel to send a tank division to help his defences there. By this act he seriously reduced the strength of his forces on the southern front and now relied very much on the Italian troops. In his diary he recorded:

> *In the evening I received reports on the Panzer Army's supply situation. It was absolutely desperate. That day we had fired off 450 tons of ammunition. Only 190 tons had arrived, brought by three destroyers to Tobruk. We only had 35 serviceable tanks left. This, then, was the moment to get back to the Fuka line.*

The "Fuka line" was a position 50 miles west of El Alamein, near the small coastal town of Fuka. Once at Fuka he hoped to regroup his forces and then conduct an orderly withdrawal back to a port on the coast, from where his forces could be evacuated across the Mediterranean to Italy. Rommel had decided that as his army withdrew he would fight delaying actions in as many intermediate positions as possible, forcing Montgomery to bring up his artillery each time, thus keeping it on the move. By this strategy, Rommel was sure that he could prevent a major battle taking place, and instead just fight small skirmishes. Rommel knew he may have lost the battle in North Africa, but at least he would still have most of his army intact to fight another day.

On the morning of 3 November, Rommel ordered one of his Officers, Lieutenant Berndt, to send a report to Hitler's HQ and tell the Fuehrer that the war in North Africa was probably lost and that he was withdrawing his army. At about midday, after visiting the front line to see how the battle was progressing, Rommel returned to his command post. As he was being driven back to his HQ his car was caught up in some heavy bombing by Allied aircraft. It was only by some skilful manoeuvring from his driver that he made it back to HQ alive.

At 1330 hours Rommel received an order from Hitler that shocked him deeply:

To Field Marshal Rommel.
In the situation in which you find yourself there can be no other thought but to stand fast and throw every gun and every man into the battle. The utmost efforts are being made to help you. Your enemy, despite his superiority, must also be at the end of his strength. It would not be the first time in history that a strong will has triumphed over the bigger

BATTALIONS. AS TO YOUR TROOPS, YOU CAN SHOW
THEM NO OTHER ROAD THAN THAT TO VICTORY OR
DEATH.
ADOLF HITLER.

Rommel was devastated when he read this. To him, the order seemed to ask the impossible. He said later that for the first time during the whole African campaign he did not know what to do. As a soldier he was trained to obey orders, but he also felt a duty to the men under his command to ensure their safety. Rommel was particularly angry because Hitler's order questioned the bravery of his men, as well as his own. For Rommel, the courage and dedication of his troops was not an issue. He knew that even the most courageous soldier could be killed by a bomb, and the level of bombing to which his troops were being subjected was impossible to defend against with little or no ammunition and hardly any fuel for tanks. As far as Rommel was concerned, this order from Hitler was asking them all to commit suicide.

However, although he believed that Hitler's "Victory or Death" order was utterly wrong, and would lead to the deaths of most of his men, he issued it to his troops. As a soldier Romel believed that orders were orders. He explained this decision in his diary:

I forced myself to this action, as I had always demanded unconditional obedience from others and consequently wished to apply the same principle to myself. The order had a powerful effect on the troops. At the Fuehrer's command they were ready to sacrifice themselves to the last man. An overwhelming bitterness welled up in me when I saw the superlative spirit of the army in which every man, from the highest to the lowest, knew that even the greatest effort could no longer change the course of the battle.

Still, Rommel was determined not to let the matter rest, and again he sent Lieutenant Berndt to report to the Fuehrer's HQ and explain the hopelessness of the situation, emphasizing that in Rommel's view, if Hitler's orders were upheld, the complete and final destruction of the Afrika Korps was just a few days away.

At about 0800 hours on 4 November, the Allies launched an all-out attack against the German lines. By mustering all their available strength the Afrika Korps managed to beat off the Allied infantry attack, which was backed up by about 200 tanks. Against this, the German Panzer Corps had only 20 serviceable tanks.

Field Marshal Kesselring arrived at Rommel's HQ and a bitter argument ensued between the two men. Rommel told Kesselring that it seemed to him that Hitler's "Victory or Death" order was a case of military sense being sacrificed for the sake of propaganda. Rommel said he thought it was ridiculous that the

German High Command in Berlin were unable to bring themselves to admit that Alamein had been lost, and that they would prefer their own men to die and the army in North Africa be completely destroyed, rather than confess their failure to the German people and the world at large.

After his meeting with Kesselring, Rommel drove to Afrika Korps HQ, which was housed in a dugout a few miles west of the front. There he was informed that the Italian sections of the Afrika Korps had been almost wiped out. Rommel could see enormous dust clouds to the south and south-east of the HQ, where a handful of Italian tanks were fighting valiantly against the hundred or so Allied heavy tanks. Afterwards he remembered:

> *The Italians fought with exemplary courage. Tank after tank split asunder or burned out, while all the time a tremendous British barrage lay over the Italian infantry and artillery positions.*

By evening the Italian tank corps had been completely destroyed.

Realizing that all was now lost, Rommel decided to disobey Hitler's orders and save what there was to be saved. He issued orders for an immediate retreat.

Ironically, the next day he received word about his appeal against Hitler's order: the withdrawal of the army to the Fuka position was finally authorized.

The Afrika Korps had been defeated. The Battle of Alamein was over.

Montgomery
In Pursuit
November 1942 – May 1943

ALTHOUGH MONTGOMERY HAD WON the Battle of Alamein, he knew of Rommel's reputation: he had been forced to retreat before but had still managed to launch a successful counter-attack against the Allies. Late in 1941, Auchinleck's forces had pushed Rommel's back across North Africa, but in January 1942, the German Commander had counter-attacked and had in turn pushed the Allied forces almost as far as Alexandria. Montgomery was determined that this situation wouldn't be repeated.

Rommel's forces had stopped their initial retreat at El Agheila, and were digging in preparation for a defensive battle. Although the superior strength of the 8th Army and the heavy bombing raids by the RAF had led to Rommel's defeat at Alamein, Montgomery knew that it had also largely been caused by Rommel's lack of supplies. It was important that the same thing didn't happen to his own 8th Army, so as his troops pursued Rommel across North Africa, he insisted that his forward division did not go any faster than his supply vehicles.

It was also important that the RAF, a vital part of Montgomery's strategy, had enough supplies to keep up their raids on Rommel's positions. That meant building airfields as the Allies advanced, so that the RAF fighter planes could take off and land near the enemy's position and not have to use precious fuel just to get to the fighting front.

All this meant that there would be no speedy pursuit of Rommel, just a steady, cautious, dogged chase, aimed at gradually wearing the German leader down. Montgomery was taking no chances. At this speed it would be mid-December before the 8th Army would have enough supplies and ammunition at El Agheila to be able to launch an all-out attack against the dug-in forces. In the meantime, Montgomery continued to send the RAF on bombing raids to attack Rommel's supply lines.

Throughout November and the first part of December, Montgomery sent out reconnaissance parties by land and air to report on the situation at El Agheila. Then, on 11 December, now certain that he had enough supplies and reinforcements at his disposal, Montgomery brought his forces up and launched two days of intense bombardments on Rommel's position.

These attacks proved too much for the Afrika Korps. If they stayed where they were they would be blown to pieces; so on 14 December, Rommel ordered his men to withdraw in small groups. Montgomery immediately ordered his troops to give chase. Fighting was intense, but by 16 December, Montgomery had destroyed 20 enemy tanks and taken 500 prisoners. The Allied pursuit continued as the Afrika Korps withdrew.

The badly damaged Afrika Korps' next stop was Beurat, where once again they dug in, ready to fight a defensive action. But Montgomery still wasn't ready to launch a full-scale attack – his supply vehicles had not yet caught up with his front-line troops. And all the time the RAF continued to bomb their opponent's position and attack their supply lines.

Montgomery's pursuit of Rommel lasted for five months. At each stage of the pursuit, the pattern was repeated: Rommel would dig in, waiting for Montgomery to launch an attack. Montgomery would wait until his supplies were fully in place, then issue orders for an offensive. Rommel would immediately retreat, hoping this time that Montgomery would follow him at speed with a strung-out force against which Rommel could launch a counter-attack. Instead, while Rommel's forces were retreating, Montgomery launched minor skirmishing attacks as he waited for his supplies to be fully restocked. When he was sure that he had sufficient ammunition, supplies and reinforcements to succeed, he ordered the RAF and the heavy artillery guns of the 8th Army to bombard Rommel's position before launching another ground attack. When this attack came, Rommel retreated ... and so the same story was repeated over and over again right across North Africa.

By April 1943, Montgomery's 8th Army had pushed Rommel's forces almost 2,000 miles west from El Alamein. They had now been joined by the combined American-British Operation-Torch forces that had landed on the coast of North-West Africa the previous November.

At the time of the Allied sea invasion, this part of Africa was controlled by the French Vichy Government. France had been occupied by Germany since 1940 and the Government itself was effectively under Hitler's control. However, most of the French people and troops in the German-occupied French colonies in North-West Africa were sympathetic to the Allies. By late 1942 the Germans in North-West Africa had been defeated and since early 1943 the victorious British and American soldiers of Operation Torch had been heading eastwards across North Africa.

Caught in a pincer movement between Montgomery's 8th Army coming at them from the east, and the Americans and British coming at them from the west, the survivors of Rommel's retreating Afrika Korps found themselves trapped at Tunis on the North African coast. The remains of the defeated army had hoped to escape to Italy across the Mediterranean, but were unable to get away by sea because the RAF and the Royal Navy had blockaded all the Tunisian ports.

For almost a month, the remnants of Rommel's army, (mainly Germans) fought a last stand against ever-increasing odds as the Allied forces bore down on them with heavy artillery fire and infantry, until they were finally overrun.

Montgomery noted in his diary:

Organized enemy resistance ended on 12 May, some 248,000 being taken prisoner. And so the war in Africa came to a close. It ended in a major disaster for the Germans...

Rommel
Goodbye to Africa
March 1943

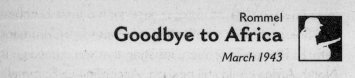

IN NOVEMBER 1942, Rommel had travelled to Germany to meet Hitler and Goering, and then had gone to Rome where he saw his wife, Lucie. He had told her that he believed if his army in North Africa was destroyed, the War would be lost and that an attempt would have to be made as soon as possible to negotiate a peace between the two sides. Rommel then returned to North Africa to continue to lead his forces in their organized retreat.

By the time the end came for his Afrika Korps in May 1943, Rommel had already been gone from Africa for two months (he had left for Germany on 9 March). The official reason was that he was recalled because of continuing problems with his health. However, in his memoirs, Rommel states that in February 1943 he had once again urged the German High Command to either increase the supplies to the Afrika Korps in North Africa dramatically, or order their withdrawal in order to save his troops. His view – as it had been for many months – was that North Africa could not be held in the face of overwhelming Allied forces, superior both in numbers and firepower. But members of the Axis High Command refuted Rommel's opinion, insisting that the campaign in North Africa could still be won. According to Rommel:

It was clear that our highest authorities were building illusions for themselves. During the morning of 8th March I decided to fly to the Fuehrer's HQ. I felt it my duty to do all in my power to rouse a true understanding in the highest quarters of the operational problems of Tunisia.

On 9 March, Rommel handed over command of his struggling army to another General and took off for Rome. There, Rommel told Mussolini what he thought of the situation, but – as before – he felt that the Italian dictator lacked any sense of reality and instead spent the whole time looking for arguments to justify his own views.

On the afternoon of 10 March, Rommel went to Hitler's HQ to make a last appeal for his army to be evacuated from North Africa before it was completely destroyed.

He was unreceptive to my arguments. He instructed me to take some sick leave. I requested to be permitted to continue in command in North Africa, but he refused.

Rommel would never return to Africa.

In an article called "Alamein in Retrospect", Rommel summed up his defeat at Alamein:

> The astonishing thing was that the authorities, both German and Italian, looked for the fault not in the failure of supplies, not in our air inferiority, not in the order to conquer or die at Alamein, but in the command and troops. The fact is there were men in high places who simply did not have the courage to look the facts in the face and draw the proper conclusions. They preferred to put their heads in the sand, live in a sort of military pipe-dream and look for scapegoats whom they usually found in the troops or field commanders. Looking back I am conscious of making only one mistake – that I did not circumvent the 'Victory or Death' order twenty-four hours earlier. Then the army would have been saved, with all its infantry, in at least a semi-battleworthy condition.
>
> The bravery of the German and many of the Italian troops in this battle, even in the hour of disaster, was admirable. Every one of my soldiers who fought at Alamein was defending not only his homeland, but also the tradition of the Panzer Army Afrika. The struggle of my army, despite its defeat, will be a glorious page in the annals of the German and Italian peoples.

Montgomery
After Alamein
May 1943 – March 1976

MONTGOMERY FOLLOWED HIS victory at Alamein with even more military successes. After driving the German forces out of North Africa in May 1943, he was made joint leader of the successful invasion of Sicily by the US 7th Army and the Allied 8th Army in July 1942. In September of that year the invasion of mainland Italy began. Again, Montgomery was one of the joint Commanders, along with the American General Patton. The Italians soon surrendered, but the German troops in Italy, under the command of Rommel, fought on. Once again, Montgomery and Rommel were pitched against one another in battle. In late 1943, however, Rommel was recalled from Italy to Germany.

In January 1944 Montgomery took command of the forces that were preparing for the invasion of western Europe in what was hoped would be the final push against the Germans. Montgomery would be working under the Supreme Allied Commander, the American General Eisenhower. Together they would plan the battle campaign to retake northern France, and then push on through France and the rest of Europe into Germany. Simultaneously, on the Eastern Front, the Russians would be launching their own offensive against the Germans.

The Allied invasion of Europe was launched on the beaches of Normandy on 6 June 1944, D-Day. On that day 75,000 British and Canadian soldiers, and the same number of Americans were put ashore under heavy defensive fire; 4,200 British and Canadians, and 6,000 Americans died as they fought their way up the beaches. But the strong German defences were beaten down and the Allied forces gained their first major foothold on mainland Europe. The Germans began to retreat across France towards Germany. In September 1944, following the success of the D-Day landings, Montgomery was promoted to the rank of Field Marshal.

The battle against the retreating German forces was long and hard, and continued right through the winter into the spring of 1945. By April 1945 the two fronts, the British and Americans from western Europe and the Russians from the east, had met and joined forces near Berlin. On 30 April 1945, Hitler – finally realizing that the War was lost – committed suicide. On 2 May 1945, Montgomery received a message from the Commanders of the German armed forces in north-west Europe that they wished to offer their surrender. Montgomery accepted the initial surrender of these German forces on 4 May, the formal surrender being made three days later, on 7 May, to General Eisenhower. It was a deeply humiliating moment for the German military. This powerful nation, which had been on the point of conquering the whole world just a few years before had been defeated and most of its cities reduced to rubble.

In 1946 Montgomery was appointed Chief of the General Imperial Staff, which meant that he became the head of the whole British army. In the years after the end of the Second World War, Montgomery's view of himself as being "absolutely right" about most things led to conflict with the British Government as far as its policy towards the armed forces was concerned. One chapter in his memoirs is called "I Make Myself a Nuisance in Whitehall". It tells of his arguments after the War with the Ministry of Defence over plans to reduce national budget for the armed forces. Montgomery believed that such budget cuts would leave the armed forces seriously weakened, just as they had been before the start of the Second World War in 1939. He held this view for the rest of his life.

In 1946 Montgomery was made a lord, and adopted as his title Field Marshal The Viscount Montgomery of Alamein, or Lord Montgomery of Alamein.

And in 1948, despite his differences with the politicians of the time, Montgomery was appointed Overall

Commander of the Armed Forces of the Western Nations. His appointment lasted until his retirement in 1958. His military career had lasted 50 years. During this period, Britain and America were engaged in a "Cold War" with the large communist-controlled countries in the east: Soviet Russia and China. It was called a "Cold War" because it never broke out into direct warfare between the major powers but each side was deeply suspicious of the other. There was always the threat that this situation would escalate into a real war involving nuclear weapons.

Montgomery died on 24 March 1976 at the age of 88. Following his death, tributes came from world leaders across the globe. Even Britain's "Cold War" enemies, Soviet Russia and China, sent messages acknowledging Montgomery's military achievements. On behalf of the Chinese communist government, Mao Tse Tung, the prime minister of China, said:

I WISH TO EXPRESS OUR DEEP CONDOLENCES OVER THE PASSING AWAY OF FIELD MARSHAL MONTGOMERY, THE BRAVEST OF WARRIORS IN THE FIGHT AGAINST THE FASCIST AGGRESSORS OF WORLD WAR II.

The full-page obituary in *The Times* newspaper after Montgomery's death said:

HE WAS, ABOVE EVERYTHING ELSE, A SOLDIER. HE WAS METICULOUS IN PREPARATION, IN ADMINISTRATION, AND IN EXECUTION. HE KNEW HIS DARK TRADE BETTER THAN ANYONE ELSE IN HIS TIME. PERHAPS HIS GREATEST SINGLE VIRTUE AS A SOLDIER WAS HIS SENSE OF BALANCE. HE WAS ALWAYS POISED IN BATTLE, ABLE TO WORK OUT HIS PLANS HOWEVER THE ENEMY REACTED.

The last word in this chapter should perhaps go to Dr Geoffrey Matthews, the historian, who wrote:

Nelson on sea and Montgomery on land are perhaps the greatest and most colourful battle commanders Britain has ever produced. There was nothing magical about Nelson's victories; they were gained by hard work and preparation long before the actual battle. In the same way Montgomery's success and the firmness of his grip upon war were based upon a master-plan carefully devised beforehand and explained to his divisional generals. If genius is an infinite capacity for taking pains then Montgomery is a very superior kind of genius.

Rommel
The Bitter End
May 1943 – October 1944

In May 1943, Rommel was sent to Italy by Hitler to help co-ordinate the Italian military. However, Rommel and the Italian Supreme Commander disagreed about how to conduct the campaign. Rommel was suspicious of the Italian Commanders and how far they were prepared to resist the Allies. His suspicions were confirmed when the Italians surrendered in September 1943. Rommel left Italy in November and his next appointment was to take charge of defending the coast of Normandy against the suspected invasion by the Allies.

Following the D-Day landings in June 1944, in which Montgomery played a key role, Rommel must have felt that he was being beaten at every turn by the Englishman who had defeated him at Alamein.

During June and July, battles raged throughout northern France as the Allies pressed on with their advance. On 17 July Rommel's car was attacked by Allied aircraft, and Rommel was seriously injured. The official report of the attack stated:

A BURST OF FIRE FROM THE AIRCRAFT SENT EXPLOSIVE SHELLS RIPPING DOWN THE LEFT SIDE OF THE VEHICLE. FIELD MARSHAL ROMMEL WAS INJURED IN THE FACE BY GLASS SPLINTERS, AND TOOK A SHRAPNEL HIT IN THE LEFT TEMPLE AND CHEEKBONE, CAUSING A TRIPLE FRACTURE OF THE SKULL WHICH LED TO IMMEDIATE UNCONSCIOUSNESS.

THE SEVERE INJURIES ROMMEL'S DRIVER SUFFERED CAUSED HIM TO LOSE CONTROL OF THE VEHICLE. IT RICOCHETED OFF A TREE STUMP ON THE RIGHT HAND SIDE OF THE ROAD AND ENDED UP EMBEDDED AT A SHARP ANGLE ON THE FAR SIDE OF THE ROAD. FIELD MARSHAL ROMMEL WAS THROWN OUT OF THE VEHICLE AND LAY SOME 20 METRES BEHIND THE CAR ON THE RIGHT OF THE ROAD. A SECOND AIRCRAFT AT THIS POINT FLEW BACK OVER THE CRASH SITE FIRING AT THE WOUNDED WHERE THEY LAY. FIELD MARSHAL ROMMEL LAY BLOOD SPATTERED AND UNCONSCIOUS ON THE GROUND. HE WAS BLEEDING PROFUSELY FROM HIS FACIAL INJURIES, FROM THE EYES AND MOUTH IN PARTICULAR. HE WAS APPARENTLY HIT IN THE LEFT TEMPLE. FIELD MARSHAL ROMMEL WAS STILL UNCONSCIOUS WHEN RECOVERED TO SAFETY.

Rommel underwent a series of operations, and in August 1943 he was well enough to leave hospital and return to his house at Herrlingen near Ulm.

During the early part of 1944, many German Generals felt that the War was lost. They believed that to continue would result in the complete destruction of Germany and instead they wanted a negotiated peace. Hitler and the Nazi leaders, including Himmler, Goering and Goebbels (the Nazi Propaganda minster and a key figure in the Nazi hierarchy), were totally opposed to the idea of surrendering. The result was that some of the Generals, led by General von Stauffenberg, decided to assassinate Hitler.

On 20 July 1944 Von Stauffenberg attended a conference with Hitler and other Nazi leaders at Hitler's HQ at Rastenberg in East Prussia. Von Stauffenberg took a primed time-bomb hidden in a briefcase. He left the briefcase against the leg of the map table in the room, just 12 feet away from Hitler. Von Stauffenberg then left the room. The bomb exploded at 12.42 p.m., killing many in the room, and injuring others. Among those who were only wounded by the blast was Adolf Hitler.

The Gestapo – Hitler's secret police – acted immediately. Von Stauffenberg was shot the same night. Hundreds of people who were suspected of being part of the conspiracy were arrested and tortured for information, then executed. Among the names extracted during torture were many of the Generals.

Some of those Generals, including General von Kluge and Lieutenant General Spiedel, had close personal links with Rommel, even though Rommel himself was not incriminated in the plot. Under interrogation, some of the Generals admitted they favoured the idea of replacing Hitler with Rommel. They felt that Churchill and the Allied leaders respected Rommel, and the best peace terms would be negotiated by him. The mere suspicion that Rommel might have been in sympathy with the plotters was enough to seal his death warrant.

Rommel's son, Manfred, a 15-year-old auxiliary in the German army, had been given permission to stay with his father at Herrlingen while Rommel recovered from his wounds. This is his first-hand account of Rommel's final day alive:

At about noon [14 October 1944] a dark-green car with a Berlin number stopped in front of our garden gate. Two SS generals, Burgdorf and Maisal, alighted from the car and entered the house. They asked my father's permission to speak to him alone.

A few minutes later I heard my father come upstairs and go into my mother's room. Anxious to know what was afoot, I got up and followed him. He was standing in the middle of the room, his face pale. "Come outside with me," he said. We went into my room. "I have just had to tell your mother," he began slowly, "that I shall be *dead in a quarter of an hour. The house is surrounded and Hitler is charging me with high treason. In view of my services in Africa I am to have the chance of dying by poison. The generals have brought it with them. It's fatal in three seconds. If I accept, none of the usual steps will be taken against my family. They will also leave my staff alone. I have been charged to put you under a promise of strictest silence. If a single word of this comes out, they will no longer feel themselves bound by the agreement.*

Rommel then summoned Captain Aldinger (who was on Rommel's staff), and told him what was about to happen. Aldinger was angry and suggested they defend themselves by shooting the two SS Generals and making their escape. Rommel told Aldinger such an action was useless. For one thing the Gestapo had men surrounding the house with orders to shoot to kill, and Rommel was determined to protect his family's safety. He told Aldinger that everything had been prepared to the last detail:

I'm to be given a state funeral. I have asked that it should take place at Ulm. In a quarter of an hour you, Aldinger, will receive a telephone call from the Wagnerschule reserve hospital in Ulm to say that I've had a brain seizure on the way to a conference.

Rommel then went outside to where Burgdorf and Maisal were waiting for him by their car. He got into the car and drove off with the two SS Generals. Twenty minutes later, the telephone rang. Aldinger lifted the receiver and Rommel's death was duly reported to him.

Later, Manfred Rommel learned that the car had halted a few hundred yards up the hill from the house in an open space at the edge of the wood. Gestapo men, who had appeared in force from Berlin that morning, were watching the area with instructions to shoot Rommel down and storm the house if he showed any resistance. General Maisal and the driver got out of the car, leaving Rommel and Burgdorf inside. When the driver was allowed to return he saw Rommel slumped forward with his cap off.

The official report of Rommel's death stated that he died of a brain haemorrhage as a result of the wounds he received in the attack on 17 July. He was given a state funeral as a hero of the German army. Manfred Rommel later wrote:

> Perhaps the most despicable part of the whole story was the expressions of sympathy we received from members of the German Government, men who caused my father's death. I quote a few examples:
> "To Frau Rommel,
> Accept my sincerest sympathy for the heavy loss you have suffered with the death of your

HUSBAND. THE NAME OF FIELD MARSHAL ROMMEL WILL BE FOR EVER LINKED WITH THE HEROIC BATTLES IN NORTH AFRICA. ADOLF HITLER"

"ON THE OCCASION OF THE UNHAPPY LOSS WHICH YOU HAVE SUFFERED THROUGH THE DEATH OF YOUR HUSBAND, MY WIFE AND I SEND YOU AN EXPRESSION OF OUR WARMEST SYMPATHY.

HEIL HITLER

REICHSMINISTER DR GOEBBELS AND FRAU GOEBBELS"

The Desert Fox had finally met his end ... killed by Hitler's SS.

Afterword

THE BATTLE OF ALAMEIN was about how two men – with so much in common but with vastly different personalities – led their armies in an epic struggle; and how the outcome was determined not just by them, but by the backing they received from their respective superiors.

Both men had strong views on how war should be fought, and both were extremely impatient at any inefficiency by their superior Commanders. Both men also believed strongly in their own abilities.

The main difference between them was in how they expressed these qualities: Rommel could be impetuous, defeating his enemy with sudden surprise acts. Montgomery was cautious, calculating, working to a well-defined plan. Their dissimilar personalities can best be seen in how they behaved with those close to them. We have seen how emotional Rommel was in his letters home to his wife, Lu. Rommel was not afraid to show his emotions, whether they were great elation or deep despair.

Montgomery, on the other hand, was described by many as a "cold fish". He did not have a close relationship with his own family, and that included his son, David. In fact, in later years, they barely spent any time together. Montgomery was very jealous of his son's achievements, and hated to share glory with anyone else. This brought him into conflict with many of those with whom he was supposed to be in joint command. Montgomery saw the American General Patton as his rival, rather than his colleague-in-arms and he resented being subordinate to Eisenhower when planning the D-Day landings. In his memoirs, he played down the positive part enacted by any of the previous Allied Commanders in North Africa, taking the sole credit for the victory. Many historians suggest he was particularly unfair to Auchinleck. In fact, Auchinleck was so angry at the way he was portrayed in Montgomery's memoirs that he threatened to sue for libel, and Montgomery was forced to publish a public apology. And when, in later years, Montgomery heard that some people also gave Freddie de Guingand some of the credit for the successful North Africa campaign, he became hostile to him and cut him out of his life.

Rommel was admired, respected and loved by those closest to him. Montgomery was admired and respected for his military successes, but not loved. When Montgomery died, despite all the titles and honours he received, he was a lonely man.

Despite having very different personalities, both men were brilliant military strategists, equally matched. But the key to the Battle of Alamein was the support each received from his political masters. Montgomery received every possible level of support from Winston Churchill. The prime minister even backed down when Montgomery told him it would be impossible to carry out a successful attack on Rommel's forces in September 1942, and the attack was delayed until that October.

In contrast, Rommel did not receive the vital supplies or reinforcements that he asked for. Adolf Hitler, although promising Rommel complete support, let his Commander down. If Hitler had allowed Rommel to withdraw when he wanted, instead of issuing the "Victory or Death" order late in 1942, Rommel may have been able to save his army, and that army may have been able to fight on mainland Europe.

Before Alamein there had been a sense among some sections of the British, both politically and militarily, that the Germans were invincible and that defeat in the War was inevitable. The victory at Alamein showed that the Germans could be defeated. As a result, morale was raised throughout the Allied armed forces, and after Alamein, the Germans never won a major battle.

The Battle of Alamein:
The Statistics

23 October–4 November 1942. (Known as "The Second Battle of Alamein". The First Battle of Alamein was 1– 27 July 1942.)

Overall Allied Commander: General Sir Harold Alexander.
Commander of 8th Army: Lieutenant General Bernard Montgomery.

Overall Afrika Korps Commander: Officially, Marshal Ugo Cavallero but in reality, Field Marshal Erwin Rommel. (General Georg Stumme commanded 23–24 October.)

Opposing strengths:

Allies:
195,000 men

1,029 tanks
2,311 artillery weapons: 908 field and medium guns
and 1,403 anti-tank guns
750 aircraft (530 serviceable)

Afrika Korps:
104,000 men
489 tanks (211 German and 278 Italian)
1,219 artillery weapons: 475 field and medium guns
(200 German, 275 Italian); 744 anti-tank guns
(444 German, 300 Italian)
675 aircraft (275 German, 150 serviceable; 400
Italian, 200 serviceable)

Casualties:

Allied: 2,350 killed; 8,950 wounded; 2,260 missing.
Total: 13,560.
Afrika Korps: 10,000 killed; 15,000 wounded; 30,000
captured. Total: 55,000.

Tank and heavy weapons statistics:

Main Allied tanks:
Crusader Mark I
Weight: 12.7 tons
Speed: 25 mph
Armament: One x 2-pounder gun; three machine-
guns

Crusader Mark IV
Weight: 14.75 tons
Speed: 30 mph
Armament: Two x 2-pounder guns; one machine-gun

M4 Sherman
Weight: 30 tons
Speed: 35 mph
Armament: One x 75-mm gun; two machine-guns

M3 Grant
Weight: 28.5 tons
Speed: 35 mph
Armament: One x 37-and one x 75-mm gun; one to three machine-guns

Main Afrika Korps tanks:
German Panzer IVD
Weight: 19.7 tons
Speed: 26 mph
Armament: One x 75-mm gun; two machine-guns

German Panzer Tiger
Weight: 56 tons
Speed: 24 mph
Armament: One x 88-mm gun; two machine-guns

Italian M13/40
Weight: 14 tons

Speed: 20 mph
Armament: One x 47-mm gun; three machine-guns

Main Allied field guns:

Size: 18 pounder
Range: 10,180 metres
Shell weight: 8.4 kilos

Size: 25 pounder
Range: 14,500 metres
Shell weight: 11.3 kilos

Size: 4.5
Range: 22,200 metres
Shell weight: 25 kilos

Main Afrika Korps field guns:

Size: 75 mm
Range: 12,300 metres
Weight: 5.8 kilos

Size: 105 mm
Range: 20,850 metres
Weight: 5.1 kilos

Sources

Quotes from Montgomery's memoirs *El Alamein to the River Sangro* by Montgomery of Alamein (published by Hutchinson & Co, 1948), reprinted by kind permission of A P Watt Ltd.

Quotes from Rommel's journals and letters from "The Rommel Papers" edited by B H Liddell Hart (published by Collins, 1953), reprinted by kind permission of HarperCollins Publishers Ltd.

Other source books:
The Memoirs of Field Marshal Montgomery (Collins, 1958)

Rommel in His Own Words, edited by Dr John Pimlott (Greenhill Books, 1994)

El Alamein by Michael Carver (B T Batsford, 1962)

Alamein by Philip Warner (William Kimber, 1979)

Alamein by Jon Latimer (John Murray, 2002)

Acknowledgements

Picture insert

1 Rommel and his plans © Mary Evans Picture Library
2 British Crusader and German Panzer tanks © Imperial War Museum
3 The German army in the Western Desert © Imperial War Museum
4 Allied sappers © British Pathe – ITN Archive
5 German heavy artillery © Imperial War Museum
6 Montgomery and Churchill © British Pathe – ITN Archive
7 Indian gunners © Hulton Archive/Getty Images
8 General Kinzel signs the surrender © British Pathe – ITN Archive

Index

DOUBLE TAKE

Two sides One story

Tutankhamun's Tomb

Carter and Carnarvon

Rivals for the Crown

Mary and Elizabeth

The Battle of Hastings

William and Harold

South Pole

Scott and Amundsen

Votes for Women

Asquith and Pankhurst

Discovering Dinosaurs

Mantell and Owen